An Emerging Theology in World Perspective
Commentary on Korean Minjung Theology

Edited by Jung Young Lee

An Emerging Theology in World Perspective Commentary on Korean Minjung Theology

José Míguez Bonino
Robert McAfee Brown
John B. Cobb, Jr.
Harvey Cox
Kwesi A. Dickson

Kosuke Koyama
George Ogle
J. Deotis Roberts
Letty M. Russell
C.S. Song

TWENTY-THIRD PUBLICATIONS
Mystic, Connecticut

민
중
신
학

The Korean characters in this book (pp. xi, 31, 115, 153, and back cover) are translated: "Minjung theology."

The cover illustration entitled "Encounter" is by Chulsu Lee. It appeared in *Han*, a book written by Suh Nam-dong and published in 1984 by Benedict Press in Seoul, South Korea.

Twenty-Third Publications
185 Willow Street
P.O. Box 180
Mystic CT 06355
(203) 536-2611

ISBN 0-89622-378-7
Library of Congress Catalog Card Number 88-72010

Dedication

Originally, I arranged to produce this volume with Philip Scharper, founding editor of Orbis Books, shortly before his untimely death in May 1985.

This book is dedicated to Philip Scharper, in loving memory of his devotion and service to the minjung.

Preface

Editing this volume has been a most rewarding experience. Working as a pastor of a small "minjung" church at the U.S. Air Force Base in Grand Forks, North Dakota, I have been deeply involved in ministry to poor, weak, and oppressed Korean wives of U.S. servicemen. Serving them for several years, I have come to realize the importance of "minjung theology" in my ministry. (The word "minjung" is a Korean pronunciation of two Chinese characters: *min* and *jung*. *Min* literally means the "people" and *jung* denotes "the mass.") My intention in this volume, therefore, has to do more with my present ministry than with my past theological training.

The purpose of this volume is to help bring minjung theology—a Korean theology of and for oppressed and destitute persons—into dialogue with the major theological developments of our era. For this reason, contributors have been chosen from various geographical regions and theological perspectives.

Robert McAfee Brown, Harvey Cox, and John B. Cobb, Jr., represent North American Protestant theologians in dialogue with Third World liberation themes, although John Cobb writes specifically from his perspective as a process theologian. Letty M. Russell and J. Deotis Roberts also write from a North American context, exploring feminist and black theological concerns respectively. George Ogle offers the insights of a U.S. Protestant missionary who has served in Korea.

Third World theologians, however, are also well-represented. Kosuke Koyama and C.S. Song write from an Asian liberationist understanding. José Míguez Bonino represents a foremost Protestant liberation voice from Latin America, and Kwesi A. Dickson writes from a reading of the Gospel informed by his West African setting.

A critique of minjung theology prepared by Herwig Wagner and the Theological Commission of *Evangelisches Missionswerk* of West Germany, as well as a response to the critique by Ahn Byung-mu and other Korean minjung theologians, are included in the appendix.

I believe these contributors represent the most eminent scholars in their fields. None of them, however, claims to be an expert in minjung theology. I have asked them to respond from their own perspectives to the English edition of *Minjung Theology: People as the Subjects of History*, edited by the Commission on Theological Concerns of the Christian Conference of Asia (Maryknoll, London, Singapore: Orbis Books, Zed, CCA, 1983), and other publications in English. They realize that minjung theology is still in the process of development. Their articles reflect their concerns and appreciation for the unfolding of minjung theology.

My own reflection may serve as an introduction for those who are not familiar with minjung theology. Although I do not attempt to provide a comprehensive summary of minjung theology, I have made an effort to help the reader understand background information, basic themes, approaches, and issues in the development of minjung theology. I have to admit that my introductory essay is both general in scope and subjective in tone.

A second voice, in addition to that of the theologians, echoes throughout this volume. It is the voice of the minjung themselves, represented by the stories that precede the essays. These stories, independent of the essays, have been gleaned from Korean history, folklore, and literature. They reflect the storytelling character of minjung theology, and speak of the anguish, hope, and imagination of the Korean people.

I am deeply grateful to everyone who has contributed to this volume. In spite of their busy schedules and heavy commitments, they have responded to my request with enthusiasm and much affection. I am also most grateful to Professor Ahn Byung-mu and his staff—Park Song-june, Kang Won-don and Lee Jong-hee—who gave me insights and empathy in my understanding of minjung theology. For the production of this volume, I want to thank the staff of Twenty-Third Publications, especially Stephen B. Scharper, who played a critical role in the entire process of publication. He not only edited the manuscript, but contributed suggestions for improving it.

CONTENTS

Preface   *vii*

Minjung Theology: A Critical Introduction
        —Jung Young Lee   3

VIEWS FROM NORTH AMERICA

What Can North Americans Learn
from Minjung Theology?
        —Robert McAfee Brown   35

Minjung Theology and Process Theology
        —John B. Cobb, Jr.   51

A Missionary's Reflection on Minjung Theology
        —George Ogle   59

Minjung Theology in Women's Perspective
        —Letty M. Russell   75

Black Theology and Minjung Theology:
Exploring Common Themes
        —J. Deotis Roberts   99

The Religion of Ordinary People:
Toward a North American Minjung Theology
        —Harvey Cox   109

ASIAN PERSPECTIVES

Building a Theological Culture of People
—C.S. Song 119

"Building the House by Righteousness":
The Ecumenical Horizons of Minjung Theology
—Kosuke Koyama 137

LATIN AMERICAN
AND AFRICAN RESPONSES

A Latin American Looks at Minjung Theology
—José Míguez Bonino 157

And What of Culture?:
An African Reflection on Minjung Theology
—Kwesi A. Dickson 171

APPENDICES

A Letter to the the Minjung Theologians of Korea
—Herwig Wagner 183

A Reply to the Theological Commision
of the Protestant Association for World Mission
(*Evangelisches Missionswerk*)
—Ahn Byung-mu 196

About the Contributors 208

Select Bibliography 211

민중신학

The Story of Ando
(From *The Story of the Sound* by Kim Chi Ha, 1972)

Ando was a young man who lived in a small rented room in a slum area in Seoul. He was unsuccessful in anything he attempted. Whenever he tried to stand up on his two feet, he saw visions of a crime he was about to commit. In order to avoid the crime, he had to run endlessly. He had to run all day and all night. As a result, Ando was restless and tired all the time.

But his trouble was more than just running and restlessness. He had bad luck in whatever he did and wherever he went. If he earned one dollar, ten dollars were taken away from him. He was robbed and beaten wherever he went until finally he was near starvation. Thus, on one evening he stood up and said, "Damn it! This is a doglike world!" Because he said this, he was taken away and beaten up by the police. He was then taken to court where he was pronounced guilty. His head and legs were chopped off, but he survived with his trunk only. The court issued him a sentence of five-hundred years in prison. In the prison house Ando hit the walls by rolling his trunk. Every time he hit walls, it made a bumping sound which made the powerful people shiver and the wealthy people tremble. This was the sound coming from the minjung.

Minjung Theology:
A Critical Introduction
by Jung Young Lee

The Meaning of Minjung

Although I and other contributors to this volume use the word "minjung" to imply the poor and oppressed people of Korea, minjung theologians have made it clear that the word minjung is unique to Koreans. It remains, therefore, untranslated. This indicates that it is difficult, if not impossible, for non-Koreans to understand fully the meaning of the word minjung.[1] Nevertheless, some attempt to explain minjung seems essential for those who want to know more about minjung theology, as several of the essays attest.[2]

According to Professor Ahn Byung-mu, one of the foremost minjung theologians, "'minjung,' like 'Jesus,' is indefinable." For him, it is a holistic, dynamic and changing reality, one which escapes categorization. Once it is subjected to definition, it becomes the victim of ideology and the object of speculation. It is, therefore, unwise to define it.

Knowing the uniqueness of this word, we should not press hard to translate it into English or any other language. What we need to do is to understand its approximate meaning as best we can. What does the word "minjung" mean, for example, to us in North America, in Europe, in Asia and in Africa? What we need to develop is a general understanding of the word "minjung" that will have some universal applicability. Let me, therefore, attempt to give a general meaning and the broader characteristics of the word "minjung."

As mentioned earlier, the word minjung is a Korean pronunciation of two Chinese characters, *"min"* and *"jung."* *"Min"* literally means "the people" and *"jung"* "the mass." Combining these two words, we get the idea of "the mass people" or simply "the people." In order to understand it in the Korean context, we can begin with its early usage. Moon Dong-hwan gives us the following description: "The term came to be used first during the Yi Dynasty (1392-1910) when the common people were oppressed by the *yangban* class, the ruling class.... At that time anyone who was excluded from the *yangban* class was a minjung. During the Japanese occupation (1910-1945), most Koreans were reduced to minjung status except for a small group who collaborated with the Japanese imperialists. Today the term minjung may be used for all those who are excluded from the elite who enjoy prestigious positions in the present dictatorial system."[3]

If we use Moon's understanding of minjung, we begin to see that the common people who have been oppressed by the small group of the elite or *yangban* (also known as gentry) belong to the minjung. (It is certainly difficult to understand this classification in a country where there are the upper, middle and lower class people.) The classification between the oppressor and the oppressed or between the *yangban* and the common people is essential for the understanding of minjung in Korea.

This classification includes the differences of social, political, cultural and intellectual conditions. If the minjung were merely a byproduct of socioeconomic classification, they would be identified with the proletariat in Marxist terminology. Minjung is much more inclusive, however, because it denotes all the common people who have been regarded as the subject of Korean history. They are economically poor, politically weak, socially deprived, but culturally and historically rich and powerful. This is what makes minjung different from the people who are only poor, weak and oppressed. The minjung are the custodians of the indigenous cultural and historical heritage of the Korean people. Nevertheless, they have been oppressed by the small elite group who have manipulated the political, economic, and educational system for their own interests. The alienation of minjung is, then, none other than the alienation of the Korean people and Korean history. Moreover, the oppression of the minjung is the oppression of the Korean people. That is why minjung cannot be understood apart from the Korean people and Korean history.

We now begin to see how problematic it is to define minjung, a reality as varied and complex as are the Korean people themselves. We begin to discern, however, the implications of the word minjung. Such implications are incorporated in the excellent working definition provided by biblical theologian Moon Hee-suk Cyris. According to Moon, "the minjung are those who are oppressed politically, exploited economically, alienated socially, and kept uneducated in cultural and intellectual matters."[4] This working definition is broad enough to include almost all the Third World people who have been oppressed politically and exploited economically by the super powers and international corporations. It is important, however, to retain both the unique and the general definitions of the word minjung without destroying either. This delicate balance needs to be preserved in the theological process.

Historical Background
Since minjung theology is a contextual and indigenous theology of the Korean people, we cannot understand it without knowing something of their background. Those who have studied the history of Korea can easily understand the long saga of oppression, poverty and dehumanization inflicted upon the Korean people by such great powers as China, Japan and Russia. For more than four thousand years of national history Koreans have enjoyed only a relatively brief period of peace and autonomy. They have lived under the shadow of powerful and neighboring countries. After World War II, Korea was divided into North Korea and South Korea. The civil war in 1950 did not attain the unity and autonomy Koreans had sought.

The Korean people are best characterized as an oppressed people, who can be likened to the "suffering servant" in Second Isaiah. As one Japanese historian remarked, "The history of Korea from its beginning to the present day is a history of suffering and destruction caused by foreign oppression and invasions."[5] In spite of the suffering owing to foreign oppression, there have always been a self-serving few who have collaborated with the foreign occupiers to advance their own interests. They became the elite or the ruling group and oppressed the majority of the Korean people. The common people, therefore, have been doubly oppressed—by the foreigners and by the elite of their own society. The primary focus of minjung theology, therefore, deals with the oppression of the majority by the elite.

Religious Roots
The religious orientation of the Korean people is best characterized as syncretism of the various religious traditions such as Sha-

manism, Buddhism, Confucianism and other new religions. Among them, Shamanism, which is also known as *Mudang*, is the indigenous religion of the Korean people and is most closely identified with the religion of the minjung. Buddhism, Confucianism and Taoism were imported to Korea from China during the Three Kingdoms period around 50 B.C.E. These religions had often been used by the ruling and upper classes to dominate the poor and lower classes. Buddhism came to Korea in the fourth century C.E. and became the state religion of Three Kingdoms and Koryo, which lasted until the last part of the fourteenth century.

Following Buddhism, Confucianism became the state religion of the Yi Dynasty for five hundred years. During the Confucian rule the distinction between the gentry (the ruling class) and the common people (the lower class) was clearly made. The distinctive characteristics of minjung evolved during this period. While Confucianism attracted males and the elite, Shamanism during the Yi Dynasty served as a religion of women and the common people.

At the end of the Yi Dynasty, the coming of Christianity and the rise of new religions marked a new age. The Japanese annexation of Korea in 1910 cast a dark shadow on the fate of the Korean people. Among the new religions, Donghak or Ch'ŏndokyo and Chungsankyo have become most prominent. They are often closely allied with the minjung struggle for liberation and independence of the Korean people from the colonial rule of Japan. Christianity, which was promulgated in Korea by Protestant missionaries in the 1880s, has been one of the most powerful religions affecting the conscience of the poor and oppressed and helped give rise to the minjung movement for liberation.

This brief sketch of Korean history may shed some light on the recent development of minjung theology. Let us now focus our attention on the emergence of minjung theology on Korean soil.

Emergence of Minjung Theology

The emergence of minjung theology cannot be understood in isolation. The temper of the times throughout the world influenced the emergence of minjung theology in Korea. The ever-widening circle of liberation theologies in Latin America and in other Third World countries in the 1960s and 1970s had, to varying degrees, a global impact. Especially for those long oppressed by totalitarian governments, such liberation movements provided a strong incentive to pursue independent courses of liberation.

Because the South Korean government censored all materials dealing with liberation movements, only a handful of Korean theologians were informed about liberation theologies. Moreover, most Christian leaders in South Korea were quite conservative and fundamentalist in their theological orientation. This relative isolation from the development of liberation theologies in other parts of the world worked to the advantage of the South Koreans, for it enabled them to develop their own indigenous theology.

Although the liberation movement of the poor and the oppressed people has its roots in the early history of Korea, we can trace the beginning of theological development through the activities of the Urban Industrial Mission in the early 1960s. Through this mission, serious Christians volunteered to work at least six months as evangelists and laborers in the urban industrial complex. While the initial aim was "spiritual" evangelization, the Christian laborers, in the face of tremendous injustices and unconscionable working conditions, perceived the struggle for social justice as part of their apostolate. In the early 1970s several Urban Industrial Mission groups were formed to combat the abuses of the workplace, and became involved in the creation of labor unions and the advancement of workers' rights issues. (George Ogle, a contributor to this volume [see p. 59], was one of those who was instrumental in the formation and operation of these groups.) In the meantime many other Christians groups, such as the Christian Ecumenical Youth Council, Church Women United, Priests Corps for the Realization of Justice, the Catholic Young Workers Organization, and the Human Rights Commission of the National Council of Churches, joined together for human rights and justice issues.

In this period of awakening for human rights and social justice, the emerging theological concern was on the minjung, the poor and oppressed mass. In other words, the evils of dehumanization and social injustice for the poor became the object of theological concern. Those theologians who had been deeply involved in the human rights movement were removed from teaching positions in theological seminaries and universities by the brutal regime of Park Chung-hee, and many were imprisoned and tortured. From these experiences of suffering and oppression, they came to empathize with the poor and oppressed mass known as the minjung.

These theologians were also able to shift their allegiance from the learned elite to the uneducated and poor. (In so doing, they received inspiration from the growing consciousness of liberation movements in the Third World, especially Latin America.) By identifying themselves with the minjung, they experienced the same agonies and sufferings as the oppressed people in Korea.

If minjung theology had been developed in "ivory towers," it would not have had any impact on the common people. Since minjung theology grew out of minjung experience, such as torture in prisons, underground movements, dehumanization in factories and farms, it has the power and spirit to strike the conscience of people and to demonstrate the liberating efficacy of Christianity.

In solidarity with the poor and oppressed majority, these theologians began to reinterpret the Christian faith in light of the minjung experience. They had an experiential understanding of Nazi-resistor Dietrich Bonhoeffer's claim that Christ stands beside the weak and oppressed in the hours of suffering and struggle.[6] Accordingly, they believed that Jesus not only sided with the poor, weak and oppressed people, but also came to liberate them from the ruling elite.

Following the example of Jesus, these theologians wanted to side with the minjung in the struggle for justice and liberation. Out of these experiences and commitments, minjung theology evolved on Korean soil.

Han as the Cluster of Minjung Experiences

One of the distinctive characteristics of the minjung experience is a particular form of suffering known as "han." Han, like minjung, is difficult to define. It is more than suffering; it is the cluster of suffering experiences. It is the repressive feeling of unjust suffering which seeks just retaliation.

According to minjung theologians, han is unique to the experience of Korean minjung, and is therefore not easily understood by non-Koreans. The closest to the experience of han is the "blues" in the U.S. black experience.[7] Han is often understood as "grudge" or "resentment," but it does not convey the same meaning. Moon Hee-suk Cyris defines it as "the anger and resentment of the minjung which has been turned inward and intensified as they become the objects of injustice upon injustice."[8] Han can be used individually or collectively to designate the unconsciously conscious layer of psychic power that entangles and oppresses the lives of the minjung.[9]

Suh Nam-dong, formerly of Yonsei University in Seoul, attempts to illustrate the meaning of *han* through stories. Let me illustrate *han* from the story of Ms. Kim, who was a skilled employee of Y.H. Trading Company. Ms. Kim joined the Y.H. Trade Union, a branch of the National Textile Trade Union, to combat the inhumane treatment and injustice to the employees. On August 9, 1979, 200 union members, including Ms. Kim, went to the New Democratic Party building to ask the government to work out a fair solution to the imprisonment of their union leader and the announced closing of their factory. On August 11, 1000 policemen intervened and dispersed the union members. During the police action, Ms. Kim was killed. She was only 21 years old and a member of the executive committee of the union. According to the letter she left to her mother and younger brother, she had, during her eight years at the factory, experienced innumerable nosebleeds from exhaustion, worked three months without being paid, and struggled with near-starvation, inadequate clothing, and worked without heat in winter. Yet she believed in the power of the labor movement. Her death embodied the *han* of eight million Korean workers.[10]

Han is the outgrowth of innocent suffering. The slaughter of over two thousand innocent citizens in Kwang-ju by the totalitarian regime in 1980 because of their demonstration against the policy of government caused the *han* in the hearts of countless bereft families. *Han* is the experience of the minjung. Collectively, the Korean people are the people of *han*, for they are the victims of foreign invasions and controls. Minjung theology is, then, the theology of *han*. Christian ministry is the ministry of *han*, and Christ came to relieve the minjung from their *han*. By releasing the power of *han*, the minjung find liberation. The method of resolving *han* is known as *dan*, "cutting off"—cutting off the vicious cycle of *han*.

Dan as the Soteriology of Minjung Theology

Since *han* is the crystallization of suffering and unresolved feelings owing to injustice, minjung theologians work to resolve the *han* of minjung. They are, in a sense, the "priests" of *han*. *Han*, however, is not sin as most Christians understand it. *Han* results from sins, the sins of the ruling group; therefore, resolving *han* is

different from the forgiveness of sin or salvation in the traditional sense. *Han* cannot be resolved without justice. As long as injustice exists, *han* cannot be irradicated. In other words, to resolve
han means to restore justice; therefore, for minjung theology, justice
seems more important than forgiveness and love. Without justice
there is no peace, no forgiveness, and no love. Justice alone heals
the wound of *han* and restores the minjung to their rightful place.

Dan means to resolve *han*. It is to cut off the chain of *han* that
creates vicious circles of violence and repression. The idea of *dan*
is dramatically illustrated in Kim Chi Ha's story of Chang Il-
dam, the preacher of liberation and of *han*, who was eventually
arrested and finally executed by the ruling group. His head was
chopped off, but strange things happened to him and to his betrayer. Chang's head appeared on the betrayer's body, and the
betrayer's head appeared on Chang's body.[11] Chang's *han* is resolved through *dan*.

According to Kim Chi Ha, *dan* has two dimensions: self-
denial at a personal level, and a curtailing of the vicious circle of
revenge at a social level.[12] At the personal level self-denial or
self-sacrifice can cut off *han*. Kim Chi Ha himself is identified as
a priest of *han*. He describes self-sacrifice as *dan* in the following
manner: "I separate my body and mind from every comfort and
easy life, circles of petit bourgeois dreams, and secular swamps
without depth. This is the total content of my faith—I know that
only vigorous self-denial is my way. Let us leave as a wayfarer,
leaving everything behind....The delusion is finished, 'Ah, a sad
and painful act of a spider which goes up in a single line in the
air....'"[13] His self-sacrifice is the only way to cut off *han*. On social and collective levels, however, *dan* can work toward the
transformation of the secular world. *Dan* can sublimate the entire
human society to the higher level of existence. Then society becomes just and *han* disappears from the world. Kim Chi Ha makes
use of Ch'ŏndokyo's (Heavenly Way) central idea of *Innaech'ŏn* or
"humanity is heaven" to interpret the social and individual revolution. In this kind of revolution, "the bottom is heaven so that
turning the bottom up is to realize the justice of heaven."[14] The
revolutionary process takes place in four stages: "Worshipping
the divine embodiment" (*Shin-ch'ŏnju*), "Nurturing the divine
embodiment" (*Yang-ch'ŏnju*), "Practicing the divine embodiment"
(*Haeng-ch'ŏnju*), and "Transcending the divine embodiment"

(*Sang-ch'ŏnju*).[15] These four stages are taken from Ch'ŏndokyo (Heavenly Way) and applied to the Christian idea.[16] The first stage is to realize God in our heart. This realization motivates us to worship God. The second stage is to allow the divine consciousness to grow in us. The third stage is to practice what we believe in God. This stage marks our struggle to overcome the injustice of the world through the power of God. The final stage is to overcome the injustice through transforming the world. In this stage resurrection takes place from death and the coming of the Kingdom of God is realized on earth. *Dan*, then, works in these four stages to resolve *han*. This is the process of salvation in minjung theology.[17]

As we said, the major theme of minjung theology is the minjung and their experience. Minjung are the people of God, and their experience of suffering owing to the injustice of the ruling group has to be eliminated from this world. Therefore, the act of liberation becomes the central focus of minjung theology. Moreover, the realization of the fruits of liberation produces the establishment of the Messianic Kingdom or the Reign of God on earth. The power of God that liberates the minjung and establishes the Messianic Kingdom is manifest in the activity of the Holy Spirit. We can thus address three main themes of minjung theology: the liberating event of Jesus Christ, the movement of the Holy Spirit, and the Messianic Kingdom.

The Centrality of the Jesus-Event

Of central importance to minjung theology is not the kerygma, the early church's proclamation of the gospel, but the Jesus-event. The kerygma, which was formulated after the event of Jesus, was intended by the early church to unify the message of the New Testament.[18] Whereas the Jesus-event is holistic, dynamic and changing, the kerygma is ideological, static and unchanging. In this respect, minjung theology is based on the Jesus-event, while traditional Western theology is based on the kerygma. The Jesus-event presently takes place in Korea through the presence of the living Christ, which Suh Nam-dong called the movement of the Holy Spirit. A project of minjung theology thus becomes the correlation of the Jesus-event in Judea two thousand years ago with the Jesus-event in Korea yesterday and today.

What, then, is the Jesus-event? It is the liberating event, the event of suffering, death and resurrection. Through the suffering, death and resurrection of Jesus, the *ochlos* of Mark's gospel, which is close to the meaning of minjung, have been liberated. Therefore, the Jesus-event means the liberating event. Whenever there is a liberating event, there is the presence of the living Christ. The history of liberating struggle must be seen from the perspective of this Jesus-event.

Although the experience of the 1970s was the focus of minjung struggle for liberation—the manifestation of the Jesus-event—this experience has become the pivot from which the past and future have been perceived, just as the exodus can be viewed as the focal point of Judaism.

Minjung theology, therefore, attempts to identify the various past events of minjung struggle for liberation as the manifestations of the Jesus-event. Some of the well-known events of minjung struggle for liberation can be traced all the way back to the twelfth century with the uprising of the Mangyi and Mangsoyi in the peasant rebellion during the Koryo period (1176 C.E.) and the rebellion of Manchuk for the liberation of slaves in 1198 C.E. In the nineteenth century, the Hong Kyung-rae peasant rebellion in 1811, the Imsul rebellion in 1862, and the Donghak (Ch'ŏndokyo) rebellion in 1894-95 were important events of the minjung struggle for liberation. The March First Independent movement in 1919, the April Student Revolution in 1960, and Kwang-ju revolt on May 18, 1980—all have been regarded as most significant events for minjung liberation.[19]

How can minjung theologians claim that all these events are manifestations of the Jesus-event? The Jesus-event is the archetype of all other liberation events, according to minjung theology. This archetype of liberation struggle is manifested in Korea through the presence of the living Christ, embodied in the movement and activities of the Holy Spirit. The importance of the Jesus-event is understood not only through the study of the historical Jesus in the gospel, but also through the cosmic Christ who acts in the Holy Spirit. The movement of the Holy Spirit, therefore, is also a central theme for minjung theology.

The Movement of the Holy Spirit

Ahn Byung-mu's interest in the historical Jesus and the Jesus-event in Mark is complemented by Suh Nam-dong's interest in the movement of the Holy Spirit. The Jesus-event, which was manifested

in liberating movements, had been taking place in Korea long before the first Christian missionary set foot on Korean soil. This
was possible because of the movement of the Holy Spirit. The
spiritual presence of God is presupposed in the liberating movement of the minjung. God as the Holy Spirit is more relevant to
minjung theologians than God as the Father or as the Son. The God
who works in us and in acts of liberation in the past, present and
future is best understood as the Holy Spirit.

Because God works as the Holy Spirit, God's work is not confined by time or space. The Holy Spirit is ever present throughout
history. What happened in the twelfth century in Korea can thus
be regarded as the work of the Holy Spirit. Coming out of the Korean cultural background, minjung theology is tinctured by the
Shamanistic worldview. According to Shamanism, everything is
regarded as the manifestation of the Spirit or spirits. The spiritual presence is known everywhere. Unrestricted by time and space,
emphasis on the activity of the Holy Spirit makes minjung theology easily adaptable to various cultural and religious forms existing in Korea. Nevertheless, it is interested in the ahistorical
character of Christianity. The "pneumatological" or "spiritual"
approach makes Christianity truly universal and inclusive.

By stressing the importance of the Holy Spirit, minjung theology rejects an undue emphasis on christology. The christo-centric
approach to theology is closely allied with traditional Western
theology. As Suh Nam-dong comments, "I call this the pneumatological historical interpretation, which I would contrast with the
traditional christological interpretation."[20] The pneumatological
approach to history is justified in light of the idea of millennium
as the ultimate symbol of the Kingdom of God. Suh Nam-dong,
following the interpretation of Joachim of Floris, reintroduced the
idea of millennium which would manifest itself in the third age
of the Holy Spirit, who surpasses the Son.[21] According to this approach, the trinitarian hierarchy as the Eastern Orthodox have
conceived it is completely reversed. It is not the Father who surpasses the Son, but the Son who surpasses the Father. Moreover, it
is not the Son who surpasses the Spirit, but it is the Spirit who
surpasses the Son and the Father.

This new trinitarian principle is an interesting development
which can be understood as a reaction against the conciliar decisions of Constantinian Christianity. Minjung theology is, there-

fore, pre-Constantinian and pentecostal in some sense. The Constantinian Christianity is the religion of the ruling group and the religion of domination. Minjung theology is a counter-movement against such a faith. Furthermore, the movement of the Holy Spirit was the beginning of the Christian Church. It was the power of the Holy Spirit that moved the hearts and minds of the people. Likewise, it is the power of the Holy Spirit that carries out the work of justice and liberation for the poor and the oppressed. The Jesus-event is carried out by the power of the Holy Spirit. Without this power the Jesus-event remains only a distant occurrence of the historical past.

Because of the movement of the Holy Spirit, the direct revelation of God, according to minjung theology, is available in Korea and in other places without explicit connection with or reference to Christian tradition. Because the act of God manifests itself in the Spirit, any act that implies the liberation of the minjung from oppressive situations can be understood as the Jesus-event or the act of God. In this understanding, institutional Christianity loses significance. What is important for minjung theology is the direct act of the Holy Spirit for the liberation of the minjung and their *han*. The world is more important than the so-called church, for the church is designed to foster the world of justice. That just world is symbolized in the Messianic Kingdom.

The Messianic Kingdom and the Millennium

The coming of the messiah for the establishment of God's rule on earth is a vital theme in minjung theology. The only nonviolent hope that the poor and weak have is the advent of the messiah or the righteous ruler who comes to restore justice and establish the Messianic Kingdom.

According to Suh Nam-dong, the symbol of the Messianic Kingdom is more closely associated with the idea of the millennium than that of the Kingdom of God. "Consequently," he argues, "while the Kingdom of God is used in the ideology of the ruler, the millennium is the symbol of the aspiration of the minjung."[22] The idea of the Kingdom of God has become so abstract and nonpolitical that it has actually been used to oppress the poor and the weak. In this respect, the idea of millennium, which emphasizes *this* world, is much more closely associated with the original idea of the Messianic Kingdom that the early Church associated with the second coming of Christ. Minjung theologians stress that the Kingdom of God that Jesus preached was never meant to be an other-worldly place or an after-life reality. It was meant to be a concrete and real world where justice and the love of God would be actualized in real-life situations.

The Messianic Kingdom which minjung theology depicts seems to be closely related to the traditional Judaic belief in the historical restoration of the Davidic Kingdom in Israel. Nevertheless, this kind of messianic hope could easily become a "nationalistic messianism" or "political messianism" when the centrality of the minjung or the poor and oppressed majority is forgotten. Political messianism is based on the ideology of rulers, while the messianic politics, or the true messianism, is based on the servanthood of minjung. A clear distinction between ruler-messianism and minjung-messianism or between political messianism and messianic servanthood has to be made.[23] The false messiahs, who represent the political messianism, are the emperors, the communist leaders, and the military technocrats.[24] Jesus is the true messiah, but he did not actualize the Messianic Kingdom while he was on earth. Its actualization is implicit in his second coming. This is closely related to the Christian hope of the millennium. Minjung theologians, therefore, stress the second coming of Christ. With the second coming of Christ, the millennium or the Messianic Kingdom will be established on earth.

Methodological Questions

Like most Third World theologies, minjung theology is a contextual theology. It is essentially a reflection on the praxis of the minjung's struggle for liberation. Moreover, of central importance for minjung theology is sociopolitical hermeneutics. It is often called the "social biography of the Korean minjung." This kind of theology is often categorized as theology from "below," rather than theology from "above." Minjung theologians, however, prefer the word "induction" in defining their methodology.

Inductive Method

Minjung theology makes use of the process of induction. The inductive process is quite different from the deductive process that most traditional theologies of the West have used. According to the deductive method, a general and universal principle of reality is presupposed. For example, theological presuppositions based on absolute truth dominate the theological enterprise. These theologies are controlled abstract assumptions. In reality, the whole theological work is based on ideological assumptions. Because theology has traditionally been the preserve of the wealthy class, this kind of theology became an instrument of the ruling group to dominate the poor and the weak. Minjung theology, therefore, proposes an inductive process, which does not presuppose any conditions or assumptions. It is simply a reflection on the Jesus-event, the event of a liberating movement. In other words, it is not an ideology or an intellectual assumption, but the concrete event of liberating struggle, that becomes the basis of theological work.

Because actions are more important than concepts, minjung theology begins with the actual event of God's act, the Jesus-event which is manifested in the many different forms of liberating struggle in Korea. One of the most important acts of God in the liberation of the minjung is the Donghak messianic movement, which has almost become the prototype of all liberating movements in Korea.[25] God's liberating act took place in the Donghak rebellion against the oppressive Japanese rule. It was the minjung revolt against tyranny. It is certainly similar to the revolt of the Jewish slaves against the Pharaoh's rule. Because the Donghak rebellion is seen as the act of God in the liberation of the minjung, Donghak or Ch'ŏndokyo becomes very important in minjung theology. As we have already seen, Kim Chi Ha as well as Suh Nam-dong attempt to synthesize Christianity and Donghak to construct minjung theology.

Because minjung theology makes use of the inductive process, the act of liberation is the starting point of theological reflection and speculation. God is known only in act, the act of liberating the poor and oppressed. An actual event of a liberating movement reveals the nature of God. In this respect, the inductive method of doing theology for minjung entails not speculation but storytelling.

Storytelling Method

Minjung theology can be best understood as a storytelling theology. Stories about the actual events for liberation or of liberation form the contents of this theology. The minjung, lacking conventional education, use stories to understand how God is acting in their lives. In the Hebrew Scriptures, God is revealed to the people of

Canaan and Galilee, and God's revelation is known through stories. In the Christian Scriptures, we notice that the Gospels are primarily the stories of what God has done through Jesus Christ. Our theological speculations are then based on these stories told by the common people who believed in Jesus. In other words, the so-called theology of the past was actually interpretation of these stories about God's actions in human history.

Minjung theology includes the two types of stories: the *silhwa,* or "the real story," and *mindam,* or folk tales. It is not always possible to distinguish between them. Minjung theologians use the folk tales as a means of understanding minjung experience. These stories are told and sung at mask dances (*talch'um*), Korean opera (*pansori*), or the Shamanistic rituals (*kut*). Both *silhwa* and *mindam* are effective tools that disclose the intimate feelings, profane language, and oppressive conditions of minjung in a realistic way. The stories convey the cultural as well as the sociopolitical biography of the minjung.[26]

There are also two ways of telling the stories: in public and in secret. Public stories are told by the ruling group in newspapers and on radios, but the clandestine stories are spread by word of mouth. The true story of minjung cannot be told by the oppressive rulers whose interest is to manipulate and control the minjung by distorting actual stories. The true stories of minjung involve the inhumane condition of teenage factory workers, the torture of court-martialed students, the abuse of political prisoners, and the suffering of the marginalized and outcast minjung in Korea. These true stories are concealed by the officials and censored in the newspapers. According to Moon Hee-suk Cyris, in Korea roughly 80 percent of the rumors are more accurate than is the news itself. By spreading the "rumors" minjung come to know the real truth. The rumors are the true stories of the minjung.

As in the case of Jesus, the real story was no doubt spread through rumors. Jesus was with the outcasts, prostitutes and oppressed people. These persons probably told stories about Jesus secretly among themselves. The real story of Jesus was, perhaps, never told by the ruling group of Jewish people or the Romans at that time. What they wanted was to spread false stories about Jesus in order to manipulate the crowd. The true story of Jesus and his resurrection was told secretly. Under an oppressive society the true story of suffering is known only through these secret rumors.

Minjung theology, therefore, makes use of rumors as the way of telling the real stories of the minjung experience.

In this way the liberating events and the experience of the suffering minjung have been told in stories, not in systematic and dogmatic theologies. If traditional theology is transcendental and deductive, storytelling theology is immanent and inductive. The former is the theology of rulers, while the latter is the theology of minjung.[27]

The Reversal of Traditional Approaches

Minjung theology, following the approach of other Third World theologies, is challenging the long tradition of Western approaches to theology. The strong emphasis on social, political and cultural elements in theology has produced a somewhat new typology.[28] In minjung theology the culture of minjung has a tendency to transform the image of Christ (rather than Christ transforming the culture) to meet the needs of the cultural adaptation of Christianity and the structural reform of society to liberate the minjung.

Minjung theology, then, reverses the two roles of traditional understandings of history and culture: the role of the ruling group and the role of Christ. Minjung theology reverses the traditional notion that the ruling class has been the norm and subject of history.

Although minjung theology does not explicitly use the Marxist analysis of social and economic categories, the reversal of the role of minjung means the reversal of traditional social, economic, and political orders. It is not possible for the minjung or the oppressed and the poor to become the subject of history and the norm of culture without reforming social and political structures. In other words, the authentic liberation of the minjung is not possible within the existing structure that oppresses the minjung. In this respect, various liberation techniques that make use of the symbolic transcendence of human existence in mask dances, Shamanistic rituals or *pansori* (traditional opera) cannot be the tools for the realistic solution of minjung liberation. This is why minjung theology is more closely allied with the ideology of Marxism than that of capitalism. When the poor become the subject, the rich then become the object. It is not reasonable to believe that both the poor and the rich become subjects since the existence of a subject presupposes that of an object. The reversal of the minjung's role in history thus means the reversal of the role of the elite in sociopolitical structure. In the final analysis, minjung theology, like Latin American liberation theology, cannot avoid the Marxist analysis of the socioeconomic structures.[29]

On the other hand, minjung theology attempts to reverse the traditional idea of salvation history. Historically, Christ has been regarded not only as the subject of salvation history but as the subject of personal existence. Christ as the "I" or the subject of human existence leads to the centrality of salvation history.[30] Minjung theology, however, reverses this idea. According to minjung theology, the minjung become the subject of salvation history and Christ the object of it by identifying himself as the servant of the minjung. Minjung theology, in this respect, interprets the servanthood of Christ liberally. Christ, the incarnation of God, is the servant who comes to serve the poor, the oppressed and the outcast.[31] Christ came to serve the minjung and identified himself as one of the minjung.[32] In Suh Nam-dong's view, the minjung take the role of master and Christ the role of servant: "In the case of minjung theology Jesus is the means for understanding the minjung correctly, rather than the concept of 'minjung' being the instrument for understanding Jesus."[33] Although Ahn Byung-mu's position is to identify Jesus with the minjung, this reversal of roles between Christ and the minjung seems to be a key to understanding the basic methodological implication of minjung theology, the cultural transformation of the image of Christ.

Compared with Latin American liberation theology, minjung theology seems to be more inclusive and holistic. Although the oppressed mass in the Latin American situation cannot be classified purely in terms of social, economic, and political categories,[34] the use of Marxist analysis by the Latin American liberation theologians gives the impression, to me at least, that their indigenous religious and cultural elements have not been extensively explored in their theological task. The strength of minjung theology is in considering the sociopolitical biography of the poor and the oppressed in relation to their indigenous religious and cultural elements. The minjung are more than proletarians. They are economically poor, politically oppressed, and socially alienated, but they occupy the center of their culture and history. They are, in fact, the subjects of history.

Critical Concerns

Since minjung theology is still in the process of development, I do not intend to make critical reassessments. What I hope to do here is to address some of my concerns which are also the concerns of most of those who have contributed to this volume.

Inclusiveness

One of the most important contributions that minjung theology makes is its inclusive and holistic understanding of the minjung. This inclusive approach is based on the movement of the Holy Spirit. When theology is centered on Christ, it has the tendency to stress exclusive characteristics coming from the work and person of Christ. When theology is based on the act and movement of the Holy Spirit, however, it becomes inclusive. Almost any event that is beneficial to the world can be easily attributed to the work of the Holy Spirit. God as the Holy Spirit is revealed in many cultural and religious contexts. Minjung theology, therefore, attempts to include indigenous cultural and religious elements as parts of divine revelation.

A danger, however, is inherent in the holistic and inclusive approach to minjung theology. It is not an easy task to include in the theological process those cultural and religious elements which are not part of the Christian tradition. The integration of Buddhist, Taoistic, Confucian and Shamanistic elements into Christian theology takes extreme caution and care. This kind of endeavor may easily lead to a movement similar to the Radhakrishnan tendency that regards every religious expression as the manifestation of the same God, or it may lead to the danger of an undesirable syncretism. We have learned a lesson from the previous attempt to integrate Shamanism, Confucianism, and Buddhism, which led to the creation of a new religion known as Donghak or Ch'ŏndokyo. Minjung theology must exercise great care and caution to avoid the danger of creating a new religion by including non-Christian elements in its theological task. It is a most sensitive and difficult task to bring indigenous elements into Christian theology without sacrificing the unique and basic characteristics of Christianity. I see some hasty attempts to integrate Shamanism (*Mudang*) in minjung theology.[35]

Source of Authority

Theology has to be contextual; therefore, the source of theology has to be based on contextual expressions. In minjung theology, like most Third World theologies, the abstract ideas or theories are of less concern than are concrete experience and praxis. The experience of minjung, according to minjung theology, is the norm of theology. In other words, minjung theology takes its source of authority from the minjung experience. The traditional idea of the source of authority, or "the house of authority," is based on the hierarchical structure. Any liberation theology which stresses contextual significance seems to be in favor of supporting the reversal of the traditional approach to the source of authority.[36]

The danger lies in making the minjung experience the absolute norm of theology. Traditionally, Scripture and tradition have been the norms of Christian theology. John Wesley, for example, adding both reason and experience, provided four sources of authority and guidelines for the theological enterprise. Among them the authority of the Scripture has been made paramount. And this approach is not confined to the Wesleyan tradition. The elevated status of sacred texts is found not only in sundry Christian traditions, but also in most of the major world religions. My concern is, therefore, that minjung theologians tend to subordinate scriptural authority and to use Scripture to support minjung experience as the norm of theological work.[37]

If experience, the experience of minjung, becomes the norm of the theological task, we have to admit that all the experience of minjung, whether it is moral or immoral, good or evil, is holy and sacred. In other words, *han* is a Korean religious experience, which, in fact, becomes more important than biblical revelation. This tendency of minjung theology to absolutize the experience of context is strongly suggested in the work of Suh Nam-dong, who had been, before his death, one of the most influential theologians in the formation of minjung theology. Absolutizing the context over the universal norm of divine revelation through Christ in history, in fact, makes minjung theology exclusive rather than inclusive. This is the danger that minjung theologians must avoid. The challenge for minjung theology is to bring both the minjung experience and divine revelation through Christ in history together in such a way that the normativeness of scriptural authority is preserved in the theological enterprise.

One-Sidedness
Another concern is the inclination of most minjung theologians to romanticize or idealize the minjung. They depict the minjung as

innocent and sinless. They imply that those who commit sin are the rulers, not the minjung. For minjung theologians, sin belongs to sociopolitical categories, not personal categories. If the minjung are holy and innocent, certainly the experience of minjung can become the norm of theology. But the minjung are not without sin. They have the same tendency as the ruling group to dominate and manipulate the weaker members of their own group.

From my own experience of working with the minjung, I have come to realize that they are as sinful and guilty as is any other group. By stressing sin as a social category, minjung theology, like other liberation theologies, has the tendency to neglect personal sins. My concern then is the need to balance both social and personal sins in minjung theology. Emphasis on structural sins should not displace a concern for personal sins. Both have to be held together in a sound theology.

Another problem with the one-sided approach to the minjung is the idea of divine love. Scripture certainly supports the premise that God favors the poor and the oppressed persons in history. Jesus, likewise, sided with them; however, it does not mean that God's love is not universal. Denying the universal love of Christ, Ahn Byung-mu insists on the partiality of divine love.[38] The partiality of God's love seems to undermine the profundity of divine nature. According to him, God's love is partial, not preferential. I have struggled with this idea for a long time trying to understand the significant implication of this partial love of God to minjung theologians. Although Ahn Byung-mu disagrees with me, I still like to think of God's preferential love for the poor and the oppressed. God by definition has to be universal and impartial. God, therefore, loves all, but prefers to love the ones who are more in "need" of love. Just as a baby needs more attention than an adult, the weak and the poor or the minjung need God's care and support more than do the rich and comfortable. This does not mean that God does not love the rich and powerful. To the rulers, God's love may manifest itself as judgment, but to the minjung it may manifest itself as liberation. My concern is that minjung theology has a tendency to see God's love as selective. When we look at the minjung and God's love in a holistic perspective, we can see in the liberation of the minjung the liberation of the rulers as well. When the divine love is seen in light of the universal love, we can see that God's preference for the minjung works to save all humankind.

Human Rights and Anthropocentrism

Historically, the dehumanization of the minjung by the ruling class in Korea has been the primary cause for the rise of liberation movements. The most important attempt to counteract the dehumanization of the minjung was to elevate humanity to the level of divinity. The essence of Donghak or Ch'ŏndokyo was to elevate humanity to such a level. Its central teaching, therefore, deals with the idea of *Innaech'ŏn*, which says that human nature is divine. It is almost identical with the upanishadic teaching of the Atman-Brahman synthesis. A person's intrinsic nature or soul is none other than that of God. By divinizing the very nature of humanity, Donghak has attempted to recover the human rights of the minjung. This was a novel and innovative idea when the minjung were ruthlessly oppressed and treated like animals under a totalitarian regime.

On the other hand, the idea of *Innaech'ŏn* leads minjung theology to the dangers of anthropocentrism. The identification of humanity with divinity goes against the accepted understanding of the Christian faith. It has been regarded as blasphemy, one of the worst sins that the human person can commit against God. The clear distinction between divinity and humanity has always been made in the Judeo-Christian tradition.

Yet the danger does not stop at the idea of *Innaech'ŏn*. Minjung theologians have a tendency to push the importance of minjung humanity further. They seem to allude to the idea of placing humanity *above* divinity by following the teaching of Chungsankyo, one of the new religions in Korea.[39]

According to the teaching of this new religion, a human being is above the divine being. God, in other words, becomes a means to fulfill the needs of the minjung. When the minjung become superior to God, the danger of anthropocentrism becomes almost unavoidable. God then becomes the object of the minjung, while the minjung become the subject of God's salvation history. Minjung theology should avoid any temptation coming from indigenous religious teachings which espouse an exaggerated human status. A human being is not God but the *image* of God. I am, however, confident that minjung theology will eventually overcome this kind of temptation.

Concluding Remarks

As I have suggested, for the minjung theologians who are actively participating in the minjung struggle for liberation, the concerns expressed in this volume may not be as important as we like to think. They want simply to reflect on the changing and dynamic flow of minjung experience in Korea. As Ahn Byung-mu said to me, minjung theologians try to avoid conceptualization as much as possible, because it has a tendency to stagnate the dynamism of minjung experience.

In my personal encounters with Professor Ahn and other minjung theologians, I began to realize that the main difference between minjung theologians and traditional Western theologians involves their ways of thinking. The Eastern way of thinking is inclusive and organic. It stresses action rather than ideas. It is more interested in the body than in the mind. As Professor Ahn said, Western people meditate on the mind; Eastern people meditate on the body. This does not mean that minjung theology denies ideas or metaphysics. When minjung theologians reject metaphysics, they reject the metaphysics of Western philosophy. When they reject ideology, they reject Western ideology. I am convinced that minjung theology in fact affirms metaphysics, the metaphysics of change as found in the *I Ching*.[40] Minjung theology is then deeply rooted in the Eastern way of thinking, which is holistic, relativistic, and dynamic in character.

Notes

1. Recently, I had occasion to visit Professor Ahn Byung-mu and his staff in Seoul, South Korea. Professor Ahn is regarded as the main figure in the movement of minjung theology. I was grateful for the opportunity to ask questions that concerned me about the development of minjung theology. It soon became apparent to me that the theological reflections expressed in this volume are not as important as we may think to the Korean theologians who are actively participating in the minjung liberation movement. Their interest is not in critical reflection or a coherent structure of a theological system. They are interested, rather, in simple reflection on the changing conditions of the minjung struggle for liberation. They are not eager to hear criticism from "outsiders," and they want to be free from categories that restrict their thinking. Their thought evolves as the minjung evolve. Their reflection changes as the minjung change.

From my conversation with Professor Ahn, it became evident that there is a clear distinction between so-called authentic and inauthentic minjung theologians. Those who have been deeply involved in the minjung movement are regarded as the authentic minjung theologians and they constitute the inner core of the development of minjung theology. On the other hand, those who are not directly involved in the actual minjung struggle for liberation are known as inauthentic minjung theologians whose interest is no more than speculation and reflection on the development of minjung theology. The late Suh Nam-dong and Ahn Byung-mu himself seem to belong to the former.

Those of us who understand minjung theology solely from reading books and articles have failed to make this distinction. What we have done in this volume, then, is mostly theological reflection on the concepts of minjung theology. This certainly makes us uncomfortable as scholars, but we must acknowledge our shortcomings, for we have no direct access to the actual minjung experience in Korea.

2. See the essays of José Míguez Bonino (p. 157), Letty Russell (p. 75), and Kwesi A. Dickson (p. 171) in this volume.

3. "Korean Minjung Theology" (Unpublished manuscript), pp. 3-4.

4. *A Korean Minjung Theology: An Old Testament Perspective* (Maryknoll, N.Y. and Hong Kong: Orbis Books and Plough Publications, 1985), p. 1.

5. Takashi Hatada, *A History of Korea*, tr. and ed. by Warren W. Smith, Jr., and Benjamin H. Hazard, (Santa Barbara, California: ABC Clio Press, 1969), p. 142. Even though I agree with him in spirit, his observation is not entirely true. During the Koguryo Kingdom, before the Three Kingdom period, Korea was free and autonomous and powerful enough to fight against Chinese invasions. See Sohn Pow-key, *et al.*, *The History of Korea* (Seoul: Korean National Commission for UNESCO, 1970).

6. Suh Nam-dong, in fact, said, "These new hermeneutics follow the proposal of Bonhoeffer, who attempted a 'worldly interpretation of the Bible.'" See Suh Nam-dong, "Historical References for a Theology of Minjung," *Minjung Theology: People as the Subjects of History*, ed. by the Commission on Theological Concerns of the Christian Conference of Asia (Maryknoll, N.Y.: Orbis Books, 1983), p. 158. Interestingly, Ahn Byung-mu, as a New Testament scholar, attempted to provide new insights into the Gospel of Mark by pointing out that Jesus did not show so-called universal love. "He loved people with partiality," Professor Ahn writes. "He always stood on the side of the oppressed, the aggrieved, and the weak." "Jesus and Minjung in the Gospel of Mark," *Minjung Theology*, p. 146.

7. James Cone attempts to compare *han* with the idea of "blues" in the black experience in America. See his "Preface," *Minjung Theology*, p. xi. See also J. Deotis Roberts's essay (p. 99).

8. *A Korean Minjung Theology*, pp. 1-2.

9. The idea of *han* is clearly expressed in Kim Chi Ha's story of "Rainy Season" or "The Story of Sound." *Han* is a key to understanding the essence of Chungsankyo, a new religion in Korea. Minjung theology seems to be much influenced by this religious outlook.

10. Suh Nam-dong, "Towards a Theology of Han," *Minjung Theology*, p. 56.

11. The story is quoted by Suh Nam-dong, "Theology of *Han*," p. 67.

12. *Ibid.*, p. 65.

13. *Ibid.*, p. 64.

14. *Ibid.*, p. 66.

15. *Ibid.*, pp. 65-66.

16. Besides Ch'ŏndokyo's approach to *dan* or the solution of *han*, there is a Shamanistic *dan*, which is advocated by Hyun Young-hak, former professor of religion at Ewha Womans University. According to him, *han* and *dan* are opposites but unite together to resolve the conflict. This union of opposites results in a so-called critical transcendence, which is expressed with satire, laughter or humor in mask dances or in the ecstatic dances and songs of Shamanistic ritual, which is known as *kut*. In the performance of rituals and drama *han* is explored in concrete body language and relieved through the ecstatic experience. This experience helps the minjung transcend the present reality and cope with the world of oppression. With the critical transcendence, the *han* of the past is resolved, and the accumulation of new *han* begins to evolve again in the unjust world we live in. This symbolic transcendence through Shamanistic rituals has to continue for the solution of *han*. This is then the *dan* of Shamanism. See Suh Kwang-sun David, "Shamanism: The Religion of Han," *Essays on Korean Heritage and Christianity*, ed. by Lee Sang-hyun (Princeton Junction, N.J.: AKCS, 1984). See also my *Korean Shamanistic Rituals* (New York, Hague, Paris, and Berlin: Mouton Publishers, 1981).

17. Ch'ŏndokyo is keenly aware of the importance of *han* and the way of resolving it. The soteriology of this religion has to do with the study of resolving *han*. All human and cosmic problems are, according to this religion, owing to *han*. The salvation of the world is then defined in terms of *Haewon-kongsa* or the work of resolving *han*. This work of resolving *han* is not carried out by the Savior but by an astronomical change, the change of the position of earth and heaven. This astronomical change as a

means of salvation is derived from the *Book of Correct Change* or *Chŏngyŏk* by Kim Il-bu. For a detailed analysis, see my article, "The Origin and Significance of the *Chŏngyŏk* or *Book of Correct Change*," *Journal of Chinese Philosophy*, Vol. 9 (1982), pp. 211-241.

18. See Ahn Byung-mu, "The Transmitters of the Jesus-Event," *The Theological Thought*, Vol. 47, No. 4 (Winter 1984), pp. 735-761, in CTC Bulletin (Bulletin of the Commission on Theological Concerns), December 1984-April 1985.

19. The Kwang-ju revolt can be understood as one of the more recent minjung struggles for liberation.

20. "Historical References for a Theology of Minjung," *Minjung Theology*, p. 163.

21. *Ibid.*, p. 164.

22. *Ibid.*, p. 177.

23. *Ibid.*, p. 187.

24. *Ibid.*, p. 190. The minjung's aspiration for the hope of the Messianic Kingdom has been expressed in many different ways. One of the most significant developments during the Yi Dynasty was the powerful apocalyptic book known as *Chŏnggam-nok*, which envisioned the millennium with the coming of *Chinin*, the "True Man." This book inspired many Koreans to hope for the coming of a just society. Since the Three Kingdom period, messianic politics or minjung-messianism has been vividly expressed in the idea of the Maitreya Buddhism. The coming of the Maitreya Buddha or the Future Buddha was always associated with the establishment of the millennium in Korea. The Donghak or Ch'ŏndokyo revolt in the middle of the nineteenth century has been interpreted as an attempt to realize the messianic hope for the minjung. All these apocalyptic hopes are inseparably related to the messianic politics of Jesus, for God as the Holy Spirit has been active among the Korean people from the beginning of their civilization.

25. As Kim Yong-bock explains, the Donghak movement "emerged in the middle of the nineteenth century, when the Yi dynasty was progressively becoming decadent and the suffering of the people reached extreme proportions. During this time the ruling *yangban* population increased but agricultural production decreased at an alarming rate. The Japanese invasion under Hideyoshi caused many disruptions and not much land was put under cultivation....Therefore the exploitation of the poor peasants by the *yangban* was extremely severe. In this historical context, the Donghak religious movement manifested itself as a messianic religion among the common people. This may be called a truly in-

digenous minjung Messianic religion. It played a powerful role in the Donghak peasant rebellion of 1895, and in the March First Independence movement of 1919," "Messiah and Minjung," *Minjung Theology*, p. 188.

26. Suh Nam-dong illustrates the storytelling aspect of minjung theology by using the story of Anguk's husband, who was illiterate but became knowledgeable through the storytelling of his wife. One of the well-known *silhwa* is the death of Chun Tae-il. He started to work as a peddler, a shoeshine boy, and a newspaper boy when he was eight years old. At the age of 16 he was employed by a sewing machine shop at the Peace Market. He worked 15 hours a day and 28 days a month in a place where no beam of sunlight penetrated. In protest against this inhumane condition, he organized a labor union; however, justice did not materialize. Finally, he poured gasoline on his body, lit it and died. This took place on November 13, 1970, and is a real minjung story.

27. Suh Nam-dong, *In Search of Minjung Theology* (Seoul: Hangil-sa, 1984), pp. 305-306.

28. Such a typology escaped H. Richard Niebuhr in his celebrated work, *Christ and Culture*. See especially Chapter 6, "Christ the Transformer of Culture" (New York: Harper Torchbook, 1956).

29. See José Míguez Bonino's essay, p. 157. Just as Marx's dialectical materialism reverses Hegel's dialectical idealism, the hermeneutical method of minjung theology also reverses that of traditional theology in the West. Traditionally the God who was revealed in Christ has been conceived as the subject of history, for God rules history according to God's eternal will. The ruling group of people identifying themselves with the agent of the divine will occupies the center by making themselves the subject of history. By reversing this traditional idea of history, minjung theology makes the oppressed and poor people or minjung the subject of history. According to minjung theology, the oppressed people are neither the object of the ruling elites nor of the divine will. They are no longer on the fringe, but in the center of history and cultural tradition. God does not control history through the agent of ruling elites, but assists in the development of history and culture through the perseverance of minjung.

30. See my *The I: A Christian Concept of Man* (New York: Philosophical Library, 1971). Also consider Paul's saying that it is no longer "I who live, but the Christ who lives in me." Here, Christ is the subject of the person, Paul.

31. This idea is clearly expressed in Philippians 2, where Christ came to the world in the form of a servant.

32. The interpretation of Jesus' role has been a controversial issue among minjung theologians. According to Suh Nam-dong, Christ is the servant of the minjung. On the other hand, Ahn Byung-mu, a New Testament scholar, attempts to identify Jesus with the minjung. See Ahn Byung-mu, "The Historical Subject in a Perspective of the Gospel of Mark," in *Minjung and Korean Thought*, ed. by the Committee of Theological Study (Seoul: Korean Theological Study Institute, 1982), p. 179.

33. Suh Nam-dong, "Historical References for a Theology of Minjung," *Minjung Theology*, p. 160.

34. See José Míguez Bonino's essay, p. 157.

35. Various attempts such as "Theology of Korean Shamanism" and *"Mudang* as the Priest of *Han"* have been made to bring Shamanism into the process of minjung theology. It, however, needs a clear theological understanding before any synthesis of Christianity and Shamanism is to be made. See Suh Kwang-sun David, "Shamanism: The Religion of *Han,"* *Essays*, p. 57ff.

36. See Letty Russell's essay, p. 75.

37. See Kosuke Koyama's essay, p. 137.

38. Ahn Byung-mu, "Jesus and Minjung in the Gospel of Mark," p. 146.

39. The affinity between minjung theology and Chungsankyo is clearly indicated in the treatment of *han* and anthropocentrism. Chungsankyo goes further than Donghak and insists that the equality of humanity and divinity is not enough. Humans should be the master of all things, including the divine beings. See for detail on the Scripture of Chungsankyo, *Daesun-Chŏnkyŏng* (Published by Chungsankyo, Kumsan, Chŏn-buk, 1975).

40. See my *The Theology of Change* (Maryknoll, N.Y.: Orbis Books, 1979).

VIEWS FROM
NORTH AMERICA

민중신학

The Story of Kong Ok-jin,
a Dancer of Crippled Beggars
(A true story)

Kong Ok-jin was born more than fifty years ago in a very poor family. Her father was an actor-singer who belonged to the lowest class in traditional Korean society. Her younger brother was a deaf-mute. In order to entertain her brother, she learned how to use bodily gestures to express her emotions. Then, when she was nine years old, she was sold and taken to Japan by a Korean woman dancer. She was sold in order to save her father from being drafted into forced labor by the Japanese during the Second World War. In Tokyo, Japan, she worked as a maid for Ms. Choi, a Korean dancer, who later died during an American air raid. Ok-jin survived but was left alone. She became a beggar. When the war was over, she was shipped back to Korea. Unable to find her family, she joined a group of young beggars, most of whom were crippled. She learned to sing and dance the way that the crippled beggars did.

Later she found her family and married a policeman, who was killed by communist soldiers during the Korean War. In order to survive, she married another policeman. She divorced him, however, because she had to join a caravan of singers and dancers. The brilliance of her talent in singing and dancing was soon discovered by a scholar of traditional folk arts. She was put on a stage in Seoul in 1978. Her performance was a great success. But the crippled beggars were unhappy because she imitated them in her dance. They thought she made fun of them. In order to please them, she decided to cancel all her performing engagements. Yet this did not mean that she gave up dancing and singing.

A few years later she opened a small restaurant, where crippled beggars were invited to eat, drink, and dance with her. Here she began to perfect her dance of the crippled beggars. She became one of them as she sang, danced, and drank with them. Some years ago she was invited to a lepers' colony to perform the dance of cripples and lepers. At the end of her performance she joined the lepers to give them hope beyond their tragedy. Okjin is a priestess of the crippled beggars and deformed lepers and a real minister of the minjung in Korea.

What Can North Americans Learn from Minjung Theology?*
by Robert McAfee Brown

There are both negative and positive things for North Americans to learn from an exposure to minjung theology.

Negatively, the most important thing is probably to acknowledge that it is not "our" theology; that we are unlikely, for cultural, racial, and class reasons, to be able to understand it fully; that we are not competent to interpret it to others; and that as a result we had better leave its exposition and appropriation to those who have created it.

Positively, we can recognize that it is a theology indigenous to the core; that it must remain that way; and that what it can best do for us is to stimulate us to find some new ways of doing our own indigenous theology.

How, then, can we learn from the minjung theological experience in ways that will first inform, then challenge, and finally transform the North American theological experience? In dealing with this complex matter, I first engage in the risky venture of trying to highlight four emphases in minjung theology that seem to offer pointers for our own theological re-thinking; secondly, I try to look at our North American theological scene in the light of those emphases; and finally, I offer some brief, concluding reflections on the future of indigenous theologies.

Emphases in Minjung Theology
What, then, are some of the emphases in minjung theology that suggest new points of departure for our own theology?

An Indigenous Development
Our first task, fraught with danger though it be, is to try to note

*I must express my gratitude to my friend, Dr. Park Sung-ho Andrew, who, in becoming my student to do work on minjung theology, became my teacher.

some of the basic concepts of minjung, as a reminder of how *indigenous* it really is. It is important not to succeed too well in this venture, so that we can recognize from the start that we are not entitled to impose *our* themes upon it, or seek to interpret it with the categories of our traditional Western theology. Although some of this material has been set forth in Jung Young Lee's helpful introductory essay, it is important, for our purposes, to recall some of it here.

We need to be reminded constantly that minjung theology is a *Korean* theology. It did not originate in Germany or Scotland or North America or "the West." Nor did it originate in libraries, classrooms, or graduate seminars. It is not only a theology for the people, but a theology created *by* the people.

"The people" in this theology are the minjung, a term conventionally translated from its original Chinese characters as the people (*min*) who are from the masses (*jung*). But, as our Korean interpreters remind us, this is not sufficiently subtle. The term connotes what we would call an oppressed people. "All those," as Moon Dong-hwan describes them, "who are excluded from the elite who enjoy prestigious positions in the present dictatorial system."

An overwhelming characteristic of the minjung is *han*, another term that defies easy translation. *Han* appears to stand for what is indicated by such English words as anger, grudge, or sad resentment. *Han* further indicates that such an attitude has turned inward. It has thereby denied adequate channels of expression, and intensified. It is further intensified by the sad realization that when attempts are made to overcome its impact, "liberated slaves make worse tyrants." The task that minjung theology sets for itself, then, is how to deal with *han*. And the gospel, in terms of this representation, is a claim that God comes to *han*-ridden people.

The response to *han* is *dan*, which circles around the image of "cutting off." In individual terms, *dan* suggests what we might call "self-denial," and in collective terms this means cutting off the vicious circle of *han* as it permeates the structures of society. The hope must be that oppressors will cease to be greedy, and— just as important and perhaps even more important—that the oppressors will stop wanting to be like their masters. Otherwise, the net result will be that *han* is simply replicated by a new set of persons and structures.

Even these brief comments should suffice to make us aware of the indigenous nature of minjung theology.

A Theology of Engagement

The comments also serve to make clear that minjung theology arises out of *engagement*, involvement, and commitment to economic, political, and social change. It is not, as we have already noted, a theology that originated in libraries, or that can be generated out of consulting a sufficient number of theological textbooks or ecclesiastical pronouncements.

The fact that many, if not most, of the individuals and groups who have been proponents of minjung theology have been persecuted for their convictions should provide sufficient warrant for the claim that the theology is a response to oppression, and that imprisonment, torture, and job-loss are ways that oppressive regimes seek to stifle challenges to their authority.

From our Western perspective, and with our incurable desire to synthesize, we are tempted, in the light of this reality of the origins of minjung theology, to conclude that it is simply an oriental counterpart of the Latin American liberation theology with which many of us have already become acquainted.

While it is true that there are more resonances between minjung and liberation theology than with the North American style of academic theology, we need to be sensitive to the claim of minjung proponents that the comparison is not compelling to them. They see liberation in the Latin American context as centering on liberation for the victims of material poverty, and therefore as having a strong emphasis on overcoming the oppressive structures that go hand in hand with a capitalist economy. The Korean experience, they claim, is, by contrast, a much more widely oppressive situation, in which liberation is needed from cultural, social, political, and economic oppression. Their own oppression, they are quick to point out, was a reality long before capitalism appeared on their shores.

Han Wan-sang has clarified the extent of the oppression of the minjung by defining them as "those who are oppressed *politically*, exploited *economically*, alienated *sociologically*, and kept uneducated in *cultural* and *intellectual* matters" (unpublished lecture, italics added).

While it is my personal belief that Latin American liberation theologians would similarly understand the extent of the forces from which liberation must be sought, and respond that the notion of their almost exclusive emphasis on economic liberation is a narrow interpretation that outsiders have incorrectly imposed upon them, we nevertheless stand to profit from the minjung insistence on the many-faced nature of human oppression. Their own Korean situation has provided irrefutable evidence that theological engagement touches every aspect of human life.

The Importance of Story

This sense of personal engagement means that when it comes to the doing of theology, and especially the communicating of theology, the methodological principle that emerges as paramount is that of *story*. Minjung theology is not a massive "system" in which every part fits into an integrated conceptual (and abstract) whole. When we are in the presence of minjung theology, we are in the presence of narratives, episodes, and events that are reconstructed, retold and re-examined, frequently in the form of drama. Out of the dynamic of the story, a new dynamic is generated in the encounter between the tellers and the hearers of that story. (Suh Nam-dong has particularly emphasized this aspect of minjung theology.) So, as Park Sung-ho Andrew has pointed out, the analytical tool has been narrative much more than economics. "Rather than Marxist social analysis, the stories of the minjung are the tools which effectively unmask the structure of a deeply oppressive society."

The use of story, as one might expect, has furnished an effective mode of recovery of the biblical message, as a story whose very historical recital gives it contemporary meaning. Many connections between the ancient exodus story, for example, and the immediate minjung story have been established. One of the most interesting examples of how a minjung perspective casts fresh illumination on the biblical material is found in Ahn Byung-mu's studies in the Gospel of Mark, where he points out that Mark, rather than using the conventional and theologically respectable Greek word *laos* (people) to designate those to whom Jesus' message was addressed, uses instead the much more heavily-charged word *ochlos* (the outcast), a concept much closer in meaning to the word minjung. The stories of Jesus' dealings with the *ochlos* thus take on a whole new meaning to contemporary "outcasts" in Korea, and a new identification with the biblical story becomes possible.

The nature of the relationship between the biblical story and the contemporary minjung story has been luminously described by Park Sung-ho Andrew:

The basic hermeneutical task of minjung theology is not to interpret the Bible (the text) in the light of the Korean situation (the context), but to interpret the suffering experience of the Korean minjung (the context) in the light of the Bible (the text)....The minjung do not exist to support the authority of the Bible. On the contrary, the authority of the Bible exists to support the freedom of the minjung.

The Centrality of the Jesus Story
It is clear that the center of the biblical story is the Jesus story, the story of the messiah. On the surface, it is a familiar story to us, and we have heard the words many times. But when we hear the Jesus story as retold by the minjung, new things emerge that have been hidden from us.

We have already noted the new light that is cast upon Jesus' mission when we recognize that those with whom he was identifying were not simply the *laos* but specifically the *ochlos* (the outcast). We can get a further insight into Jesus' ministry when we reflect that from the minjung perspective, Jesus identified with and suffered with the minjung of his time, that he learned their *han*, and that his act of going to Jerusalem and suffering was "the act of *dan*," cutting loose from, and helping others to cut loose from, the *han* that was so stultifying.

The message of his ministry is thus a message of hope. The minjung need not remain locked in *han*. They can participate with Jesus in the act of *dan*, and secure, with him, their own liberation.

There is another aspect of the message, however, for Jesus is not the only messianic claimant on the scene, either in biblical times or in our own. The real task is always to distinguish between true and false messiahs, and the particularly enticing messiah for those with power who want to retain it, is some form of nationalistic messianism. Those who counter such a messiah with another messiah, Jesus of Nazareth, feel the full wrath of the false messiah's followers.

In this regard, Kim Yong-bock makes an important distinction between "messianic politics" and "political messianism." Nationalist messianism is of the latter variety, wherein the state itself becomes the savior, the deliverer. The Jesus story is a story of "messianic politics," in which ideologies are neither exalted nor absolutized.

Within such a perspective there are still emphases being debated (as there are in any healthy theology). Probably the most significant issue is the relationship between Jesus and the minjung. There are some who claim that the real message of the gospel today is the minjung themselves, that the messianic task is to be carried out through them, and that they are the true bearers of hope and meaning. Others stress the need to develop a clearer sense of the relationship between Jesus and the minjung, feeling that the danger of the first position is to cast Jesus in too subordinate a role in the contemporary retelling of the story. We can be sure that the last word has not yet been heard on this matter.

The Meaning of Minjung Theology for North Americans

So much, then, for four characteristics of the minjung way of doing theology in Korea. Their further refinement, the creation of commentaries and text about them, is not our task, and we will wait with eagerness as new expressions and refinements of minjung theology are developed and made available to us. What, then, does minjung theology mean for us?

Our task is not to "import" minjung theology to North America. What we can and must do is something like this: as we observe minjung theologians continuing their theological task in their situation, we must look at our own task with the same kind of seriousness, and, drawing what leads we can from them, proceed to examine our situation in such a way that a new North American theology emerges for us.

Without trying to imitate the content of minjung theology, we can take the four characteristics cited above and use them as springboards for a theology relevant to our own situation.

Building Our Own Indigenous Theology

We too need to develop *an indigenous theology of our own*. With whatever similarities our theology may finally have with other theologies, it will *not* be transplanted liberation theology from Latin America, or minjung theology from Korea, or kairos theology from South Africa. It will not arise out of those other situations, but out of our own situation.

Negatively, such a setting out of the task helps us to remember that our product will not be universal. Put more bluntly, it will be parochial, which is to say it will come from, and be relevant to, one small slice of Christian and human experience. Such a recognition may keep us from trying to foist it off on others, as though whatever theology *we* came up with was meant to be the universal theology for all times and places. We are always tempted to universalize out of the particularities of our own experience, and we need constantly to be reminded that there is not just one way to talk about the gospel, i.e., *our* way. There is no such thing as a "universal" theology. Every theology is partly a product of the culture out of which it originates, and no culture can claim a perspective that entitles it to define the whole human experience in its terms alone. That is cultural and theological imperialism at its worst.

A good test case in this area is emerging in the aftermath of the 1985 Synod of Bishops of the Roman Catholic church. One group at the Synod pressed hard for the creation of a "universal catechism" that would restate the true and unchanging content of Catholic faith in the face of the confusions that presently dog contemporary Catholic life. Another group, while not averse to a fresh attempt to catalogue the faith, urged strongly that a *variety* of such catechisms be produced, reflecting the different situations, cultures, modes of discourse, and so forth that exist within Catholicism as a whole. In the light of the minjung experience, we must surely hope that if there is to be a new accounting of the faith, it will emerge along the lines of the second alternative rather than the first. A single "universal" statement would inevitably be culture-bound by the preconceptions of those who compose it. And since it would be composed in Rome, by Europeans, we can anticipate that it would employ European, Western, classical modes of thinking and speaking, and to just that degree be irrelevant to Asians, Africans, Latin Americans, and even a large number of Europeans. Adopting the second alternative would at least pay lip service to the need for diversity of expression, and while such attempts would probably still over-conceptualize, they would at least be more regionally appropriate and less imperialistic, in both design and content, than any attempt at a single statement could ever be.

Positively, acknowledgment of the need to create "an indigenous theology of our own" will immediately mean amending the concept as thus stated. We will of necessity have to create North American indigenous *theologies*, since to speak of an indigenous North American situation means acknowledgment of a pluralism of vast proportions. The same imperialistic seduction we are decrying would be present once again if white males, who have usually carried the ball in the past, were to claim it as their task to create a new North American theology.

Fortunately, there are at least two highly sensitive and articulate groups within the American churches—blacks and women—who will see to it that this does not happen. Any North American theological venture will have to be characterized by pluralism—offering theologies that speak from and to blacks, for example, or theologies that speak from and to women. And when we add to those two groups all the others within our society who, after much struggle, are beginning to be heard—Native Americans, Asian-Americans, Hispanics, gays, lesbians, and so on—we can be sure that "theology" is in process of becoming a word that will exist almost exclusively in the plural mode.

Sooner or later, these various movements will discover that they share a few common themes, and some synthesis will become possible. But the time for that is not yet.

What all groups can do for the present is to draw on the distinctively North American parts of their heritage, and use them in the articulation of their viewpoints: the underground railroad, the suffragette movement, the conquest of the West retold from a Native American perspective, the tragedy of the Vietnam War, and so on. It will be appropriate for some groups to draw on the theme of "liberty and justice for all" (as the Catholic bishops did in dealing with the nation's bicentennial in 1976), while others might build on Thomas Jefferson's insight that America needs a new revolution every twenty years.

Engagement Over Speculation

We are already beginning to describe a second characteristic we discovered in minjung theology: Our own indigenous theologies must come out of *engagement*, rather than speculation. This is not to say that speculation is unimportant, but only that it is secondary. Obviously, we can and must speculate about what we experience, but the speculation needs to grow out of the experience, rather than being imposed upon it in such a way that significant aspects of the experience are in danger of being denied, lest the adequacy of the speculative model be threatened—a familiar route to the demise of many past theologies.

It is a characteristic of classical Western theology, however, that it has been long on speculation and short on engagement. The long speculative domination of the elite, white, male fraternity is now under siege, and it is doubtful if the rations in the redoubt will hold out indefinitely. The model is being challenged by many new models of theological understanding, which, whatever their variation, have in common the fact we have observed in the case of minjung theology: they proceed not only out of engagement, but also out of the engagement of the marginalized, those who heretofore have not had much say in, or control over, their destinies. What these groups share is not only a common history of oppression, but a common experience of the Scriptures, as the literature that came out of, and spoke to, those who were oppressed. The co-optation of these writings by the affluent and powerful is now being exposed.

This represents a double bind for those who have so long dominated the theological scene, for not only have they tended to have more affinities with oppressors than with oppressed, they have also been the self-appointed guardians of the correct interpretation of Scripture, and have frequently succumbed to the temptation to use the authority of Scripture to buttress the ongoing domination of systems of oppression. It will take considerable grace for those who have been the possessors of both social advantage and hermeneutical authority to surrender their twin points of dominance, but any sober reading of the situation makes clear that the challenges to their preeminence will be increasingly insistent and even strident. It may be that one avenue for making the necessary shifts can come through openness to the impact of story.

Retrieving Our Own Stories
This is partly because the form of Scripture itself, as minjung theology is reminding us, is not that of a textbook of systematic theology despite the attempt of countless generations of scholars to make it so, but basically a narrative, a *story*, an account of the historical experiences of a people. When asked about God, the response of the biblical writers is not, "Here is a list of divine attributes, arranged within an analogous hierarchical structure that mirrors our relationship to the created order," but rather, "Here's a story. Once upon a time there was a man named Abraham, and a woman named Sarah, and they had it made. And then one day they heard a voice...."

Openness to the biblical story does at least two things: 1) it challenges the adequacy of our own stories; and 2) it opens us to the power of other stories as well. In our North American setting, one of the most important steps we could take would be to develop a new openness to our own national story, in all of its possibilities and perversions, when seen in the light of the biblical story. The goal of the story (previously cited as "liberty and justice for all") could be one of a series of master-images, as James McClendon has called them, against which to measure the actual situation today in relation to the biblical story's insistence on God's partiality for the poor. Do we have "liberty and justice for all" if the poor are excluded? If not, are we the ones presently being denied those gifts? What are the reasons for the denial? Who are those responsible for the ongoing denial? How must our social structures be changed so that instead of providing liberty and justice for some, they can provide "liberty and justice for all"? Is it, indeed, real liberty and justice even for some, so long as it is not available for all?

The interweaving of the stories can be extended to the global scene as well. Does the foreign policy of our nation provide, or deny, liberty and justice for Third World nations? Do our policies support rather than challenge repression? How do our own economic desires impact the growing economic needs of other nations? Why do we so consistently support dictators and thwart peoples' attempts at radical social change?

At this point, for those of us in the USA, our story and the plight of the minjung come into tragic juxtaposition, for the plight of the minjung is seen to be exacerbated rather than diminished by our nation's policies. And that begins to sound like "nationalistic messianism" on our part.

Exploring the Messianic Theme
Reference to "nationalistic messianism" calls to mind a fourth minjung characteristic we can use as a yardstick for measuring our own theological perceptions. This is the *messianic* theme, understood in minjung theology as standing in a special relationship to the people, who are called upon to play a messianic role.

If there is a messianic role for the people to play, it obviously makes a great difference which "people" enact it. In Jesus' time, it was not the Herods and the Pilates who were the bearers of messianic hope. It was the poor, the dispossessed, the *am-ha'aretz*, who found their messianic hopes focused in the one who came from among them, and who championed their cause, Jesus of Nazareth. It is easy to see today, in a land like Korea, where there is massive oppression, how those who are the victims of that oppression can relate directly to a messianic hope conceived in such terms as throwing off the yoke of the oppressors, and building a new community centered on justice.

But what are we to do with such an emphasis in our North American situation? It does not take much perception, though it takes a good deal of grace, to realize that in any replaying of the biblical messianic story, the part *we* play resembles that of Herod and Pilate more than the *am-ha'aretz* or that (in terms of the Hebrew scriptural imagery) we find ourselves cast in the role of servants in Pharaoh's court rather than as members of the oppressed groups to whom Yahweh promises liberation.

Projecting this onto the national scale, we can learn from the minjung emphasis that it has always been the USA's temptation to take upon itself a messianic vocation, whether through doctrines of manifest destiny or through the exploitative mentality that causes us to support such despots as Somoza in Nicaragua, Pinochet in Chile, and Marcos in the Philippines. Thus, while the minjung lesson for Korea may be to encourage the marginalized in society to organize and struggle for liberation, the message to North Americans may be to warn us against the evil consequences of arrogating to ourselves a messianic role. A message about true messianic zeal also contains a warning about false messiahs. When we take it upon ourselves to decide what form of government is appropriate for another country, as we did in Chile and are in process of doing in Nicaragua, we are certainly engaging in a false messianic role.

The point is made with blatant clarity in the case of South Africa, where the role of the "chosen people" in the exodus story, rather than being assigned to the blacks (as every parallel would suggest), has been pre-empted by white South Africans, who thereby understand themselves as the minority favored by God and permitted to do whatever is necessary to maintain superiority over other races, and fulfill the destiny God has ordained for them alone. Clearly reprehensible when stated so baldly, the doctrine is subtly present in our North American life and experience, and just as it will take a rising sense of black consciousness in

South Africa to dispel the erroneous adaptation of the Exodus story there, so, too, will it take similar retellings of the biblical and North American story in North America from minority perspectives to thwart our own attempts to co-opt both stories on behalf of a white majority that would like to continue to use its power for its own ends.

The Fruits of an Engaged Theology

What can we expect to result from the engagement of various indigenous theologies with one another?

Initially, we can anticipate confrontation, challenge and difficulty in maintaining significant rapport. This will be true not only because different groups need to develop a self-identity denied them in the past (a reality that will lead to separatist tendencies initially) but also because marginalized groups will discover with new intensity how the dominant groups have manipulated their power to establish and maintain that dominance.

A little later, we can hope that as different groups seek to relate to one another, their perspectives will undergo some modification. As they begin to hear one another and compensate for what may have been over-emphases, they may re-think their own stories in the light of the other stories. The history of a group of Third World theologians, meeting annually over a period of several years, suggests that this is possible. Initially attracted to one another because of shared liberation concerns, they discovered that they were proceeding from very different assumptions about their societies and their churches, and only later discovered that while important cultural and historical differences will remain, they can learn from one another to correct emphases in their own viewpoints that have been too parochial.

As the process matures, tentative syntheses may emerge. This will be a dangerous moment, for there will be a temptation in each group to move toward synthesis by making its perspective and presuppositions normative for the others, and imposing on diverse materials and experiences a counterfeit stamp of uniformity. This would disclose a fresh instance of theological imperialism, from which extrication would have to be sought. Even so, to the degree that common concerns, common insights, and common programs for action can evolve, clear gains will have been registered.

What we must finally hope for is not a new theological synthesis, but a new recognition that there can be unity within diversity. This will represent a dynamic rather than a static situation. Various indigenous theologies will have to test themselves against other indigenous theologies, to ensure that, in attempting to respond to their own situations, they have not simply become parochial, and have thereby skewed the message. The situation will not be unlike that which already obtains within the World Council of Churches, where massively different viewpoints running the gamut from Russian Orthodoxy to Chilean pentecostalism find enough in common to share in mutual undertakings, significant degrees of shared worship, and an ongoing commitment to theological and ecclesiological dialogue, self-confident enough to risk constant exposure to one another, and humble enough to acknowledge the mutual refinements of position that grow out of such exchange.

In such an ongoing dialogue, the rest of us must recognize that minjung theology has become a significant and articulate partner.

The Story of Hong Kil-dong
(From the popular novel written by Ho Kyun during the Yi dynasty)

Hong Kil-dong became dissatisfied with the world in which he lived. The existing social and political structure was completely controlled by the aristocrats or *yangban* class. He ran away from home and organized a group of bandits who were to reform radically this society. He called the group *hwan-bing-dang* which means "the party that rescues the poor." He and his followers attacked the rich people and took away their wealth and distributed it to the poor. This created much social chaos and sparked a revolutionary spirit among the poor and oppressed. Yet it was impossible for the government to catch him and his bandits. Finally, Hong Kil-dong was persuaded by his father to leave the country. He went to an island known as Yuldo. This island became a paradise where the conflict between the rich and the poor, the gentry group and the common people, was eradicated through the Messianic Kingdom of Hong Kil-dong.

Minjung Theology
and Process Theology
by John B. Cobb, Jr.

As Christianity declines in Europe and North America, attracting fewer of the best thinkers and most sensitive seekers, Christianity in Asia, Africa, and Latin America is assuming new vitality. The epoch in which global Christianity centered in the North Atlantic peoples with the other continents as fields of mission has ended. We can still speak of older and younger churches. But now, as the younger churches are reaching maturity, that distinction will become unimportant. The center of world Christianity numerically, spiritually, and theologically will no longer be in the North Atlantic countries. Only financially will these still be powerful, and that hegemony, too, will fade.

One of the countries in which a younger church has become mature and ready to take its share of global leadership is South Korea. The vitality of the church there is startling to the jaded North Atlantic Christian. In these comments, however, I speak not of the dynamic faith, evangelism, and church growth in that country, but of the theology.

Theology as an academic discipline may be the last feature of the life of Christendom to cease to have its center in the North Atlantic. There is a cumulative scholarship and a history of intellectual reflection, especially in central European Protestantism, whose objective excellence cannot be questioned, and which is hard to transplant into any other soil. Whereas church life in the United States in general is thoroughly indigenized, it has proven difficult for scholars and theologians in the United States to indigenize German theology or to develop an indigenous tradition of comparable strength. In this respect the problems and challenges facing the Asian, African, and Latin American churches, as well as ethnic minority Christians in the United States, are formidable.

If scholarship and theology were as "objective" as they sometimes appear, one might argue for a division of labor. Let the German-speaking peoples continue their work of scholarly and theological leadership. Let them educate our theological faculties. That can be their great contribution to world Christianity. Meanwhile, it can be proposed, we will proceed elsewhere with what needs to be done in the life of the church according to our cultural situations.

It has been black theology, Latin American theology, and feminist theology in particular that have taught us that this solution is inadequate. The "objective" scholarship and theology of the great tradition in fact reflect their cultural context in the university and in central Europe as well as the male dominance that has been taken for granted. By its very excellence it inhibits Christians in other situations from affirming the different understanding and wisdom gained through diverse situations. It is striking how dependent on this tradition are its critics. To sort out what is valid for all from what is ideological in the great scholarly and theological traditions is no mean task!

In the United States the best known efforts to formulate new expressions of faith without ignoring the scholarly tradition are black North American theology and Latin American liberation theology. But the ferment of thought in Korea is no less important. There, too, some scholars and theologians educated in the great tradition are seeking to shift their vocation from advancing and interpreting that tradition to addressing the urgent issues of their people. Among those who have made this move the best-known group call themselves theologians of the minjung, that is, of the oppressed and suffering people of Korea.

The Challenge of Minjung Theology

If one views their work from the point of view of the central European theological tradition, one must conclude that minjung theology is more an aspiration than a reality. But this is not the only point of view from which theology can be understood. Indeed, minjung theology constitutes a challenge to re-define theology.

In the modern West, theology is understood as one scholarly discipline, or family of disciplines, alongside others. To be such a discipline it must have a distinct subject matter and an appropriate scholarly method. Theology takes as its subject matter Christian Scriptures and traditions. Its method is hermeneutics.

If one studies the writings of the minjung theologians to ascertain their contribution to this discipline, one will be disappointed. These writings have obvious theological elements, and there are, scattered throughout, interesting bits of scriptural hermeneutics. But as a whole they do not constitute a significant contribution to the task of the established discipline, for their starting point is the suffering of the minjung which is then interpreted in light of the Bible.

What are North Americans to make of this reversal? My answer is that we should rejoice. This is, indeed, the liberation of theology from its captivity to the university. Whereas in the European tradition theology in the days of its health addressed, from the perspective of faith, whatever questions were most urgent for the Christian community and for the people as a whole, the move of theology into the university, along with the nineteenth century organization of the university into disciplines, forced the narrowing of theology to one discipline among others. Much of the writing of Augustine, Thomas Aquinas, and Martin Luther cannot count as theology by these standards. The church that must look to the academic discipline of theology for intellectual guidance is severely impoverished. Academic theology is hardly able to address even the most massive and pressing issues of our day, such as those of justice and peace lifted up for focused attention by the World Council of Churches.

In Augustine we find not only an interpretation of the great historical changes of his day but also guidance as to how to think about christology and pneumatology, Trinity and ecclesiology, sin and grace. In the long run the Korean church must interpret and reinterpret all of these doctrines as well as the historical events in which it is immersed. Each part of the task should inform the others. I am confident that this will come in due course as the relevance of all these topics to the real situation of the church brings the need for such consideration into focus. Minjung theology belongs to the church, not to the university, and accordingly its purpose is to respond appropriately to the situation rather than to supply systems that are intellectually satisfying chiefly to the creators.

Minjung theology arose out of involvement in the struggle for the rights of the minjung. Hence it is shaped by reflection on the structures of oppression and of how this oppression has been experienced by the minjung. This has led to interest in the traditional culture of the Korean minjung and in how they have interpreted oppression and responded to it throughout the centuries.

Affirming Korean Culture

Meanwhile other Korean theologians have responded to different features of the situation of Korean Christians. They share with many other Christians in younger churches an inner division between their Christian modes of understanding and action, largely derived from the West, and their Korean cultural heritage. Many Korean Christians have been taught to despise this Korean heritage, but they cannot reject it without rejecting much of themselves. The true indigenization of Christianity in Korea requires a critical reaffirmation of Korean culture, not only in its popular forms but in its "high" forms as well. This means a new appreciation of Confucianism, of Taoism, and of Buddhism. Inevitably, there are mutual suspicions between those working for justice and those seeking cultural indigenization. But the situation in Korea in this respect seems less difficult than elsewhere. Already there are signs of mutual recognition between minjung theologians and those who focus on traditional culture and religion. They are allies in a common struggle for authenticity in Korean Christianity.

For the time being all such efforts must inevitably be at the fringes of the Korean church. The center is constituted by evangelical and evangelistic zeal that has little time for such critical questions. The doctrines and practices adopted from the West have been adapted to the Korean situation with remarkable success. In due course a price will be paid for the limitations and insensitivities built into this approach, and even now the work of perceptive theologians may influence the course of church expansion in hopeful ways. But it is in the future, as this phase of rapid Christian growth comes to an end, that the present theological ferment will show its greatest relevance. I hope minjung theology will be ready for the opportunities that await it.

The Mutual Enrichment of Process and Minjung Theologies

Can a U.S. theologian in the "process" tradition such as myself do more than comment appreciatively? Probably not much. I can reflect again about my own vocation, my own context, and my own methodology. And I can express appreciation to minjung theologians for their contribution to my thought.

But there is something more. Just as there are universally, or at least widely, valuable elements in the scholarly tradition of German theology and in minjung theology as well, so also I can hope that there may be elements in North American process theology that could prove helpful to minjung theologians as well as to other Christians in Korea. Indeed, I believe there are. At first glance, process theology's interest in metaphysics and cosmology seems far removed from minjung theology, but at a deeper level the gap narrows. To free Korean Christian theology from its bondage to Western categories requires reflection on the nature of those categories. Even within the West they have proved limiting and binding. Process philosophers have struggled with this problem for decades, and the revisions we propose at a foundational level have notable points of contact with traditional Asian wisdom. Process theologians have done much to recast Christian teaching in these revised categories, and the results may prove suggestive to Asian Christians who seek authentically Asian expressions of Christian faith. At the very least such Asian Christians will find enthusiastic moral support for their work among process theologians.

On one occasion Jesus is reported to have said: "Anyone who is not for me is against me" (Mt. 12:30). I know neither whether these are authentic words of Jesus nor the circumstances of their original utterance. But they well characterize the attitude likely to be adopted at certain stages in the emergence of a new theology. Those grasped by a fresh and convincing insight are likely to believe that all those who do not join them are against them. They view with suspicion even sympathetic comments by those who are not engaged with them. For example, during the period of the hegemony of neo-orthodox theologies, process theologians often fell into this frame of mind. Where certain insights that seemed key to us were not affirmed, we saw others as against us.

Liberation theologies generally pass through this phase. For example, minjung theologians saw that theology that was not sensitive to the situation and perspective of the suffering people was distorted and used to support oppression or at least to dull consciences about oppression. Only those who are engaged with the minjung can really free themselves from the ideologies of the dominant group, the oppressors. This was never meant to limit true theology to the Koreans. The close similarity of the suffering of North American blacks from slavery, segregation, and continuing discrimination generated an immediate camaraderie with black theologians. But where the identification with the minjung was not manifest, the assumption was one of opposition.

On another occasion Jesus is reported to have said: "Anyone who is not against us is for us" (Lk. 9:50). Again I cannot speak of the original reason for the saying. But it reflects an attitude that sometimes arises at a later stage of a theological movement. As the complexity of the problematic becomes apparent, there is more openness to a multifaceted and a multilevel approach. Also, there is need for allies and supporters. Sensing the power of the real opposition, one welcomes all those who do not oppose one's efforts. For example, process theologians have learned to find points of agreement and mutual support in the counterculture, in the ecological movement, in the "new physics," among feminists, among Roman Catholics inspired by Teilhard de Chardin and the Second Vatican Council, among those seeking inter-religious dialogue, and in the various movements for indigenization of Christianity and for liberation of oppressed people around the world.

As minjung theology moves into this later phase, it is my hope that there can be a growing alliance between minjung theology and process theology. Few, if any, process theologians in the United States have paid a price in unemployment or imprisonment for identification with the minjung. In that sense we have not earned the confidence of minjung theologians. But in our very different context, focused on very different issues, we have come to see the world in such a way that we hope to support and encourage those who actively identify with the oppressed and pay the price. As we seek to affect the course of events in our churches and in our government, we need help and guidance from Christians in Korea (and elsewhere) who understand, as we do not, the effect of U.S. policies on the minjung of the world. No more than the minjung theologians are able to determine the policies of Korea are we able to determine those of the United States. But we would like, at least, to be directing our efforts in the right direction. For that we need their moral support as well as their wisdom.

The Story of Chung Tae-il
(A true story)

Tae-il was born into a poor family in Taegue on August 26, 1948. Since the age of eight, he worked as a peddler, a shoeshine boy, and a newspaper boy. He never finished grade school. At the age of 16, he was employed by a sewing machine shop in the Peace Market in Seoul. There were about 20,000 sewing machinists there, mostly women. The workers' average age was 18, and about half of them were between one and 15 years old. They worked 15 hours a day but were poorly paid—their wages amounted to the sum of money that the owners of the shops spent for lunch. Their working conditions were miserable; no sunlight and no fresh air were available. In order to improve the working conditions and pay, Tae-il decided to organize a labor union. In March of 1969 he was fired because of his union activity.

Tae-il was determined to protest against the dehumanization of workers at the Peace Market. He made a resolution to give himself up for the cause of his poor brothers and sisters. He went back to the Peace Market and started to organize the labor union again. He organized the group to march on the Peace Market place. The protestors were blocked, however, and dispersed by police. Tae-il then poured gasoline on his body and lit it. He died shouting, "Do not exploit the young lives! Let me not die in vain." He died at the age of 22. Tae-il gave his life in his following of the minjung.

A Missionary's Reflection on Minjung Theology

by George Ogle

Introduction

I wish to begin this paper by expressing deep gratitude to those who, through their own sufferings, have formulated the theology called minjung theology.[1] It has a New Testament ring to it that has persuaded me of its authenticity. And, those who espouse it present such a genuine witness that I am convinced of their apostolate.

This article is, therefore, not a critique of minjung theology. Rather, it is an essay based on my experiences as a foreign missionary involved in Urban Industrial Mission (UIM). Those experiences provided me with a unique exposure to the *han* of Korea's industrial workers.[2] This article is an essay of appreciation to those who have been able to articulate the hardships, and the significance of those hardships, borne by the workers of Korea. South Korea has undergone considerable industrial development in the last two decades. Much of the credit for that development should go to Korea's workers but it is credit they never receive. Most of the sacrifice and suffering that has made progress possible has been that of the ordinary factory worker. This essay is primarily a reflection upon the *han* she and he endures.

Missionary Origins

During World War II the Germans occupied France and carried thousands of French workers into Germany as forced laborers. Among those laborers were a dozen or so Catholic priests who disguised themselves as workers so that they could continue to minister to their people. Most of the priests were discovered by the Germans and executed. A few survived.

After the war, the priests who survived, with the help of their bishop, organized the Mission to Paris, a mission to France's industrial working class. Priests became workers and participated fully in the factory and community lives of their fellow workers; some of them became shop stewards and leaders in their labor unions.

The worker priest movement, however, did not last long. Pillars of the church, rich industrialists, who resented the priests' presence among their employees, brought pressure upon the church hierarchy to curtail the worker priest movement. The priests had to decide between being a priest or a worker—one or the other. Most chose to remain as workers. In 1954 by papal decree the Mission to Paris was disbanded.

Across the Atlantic Ocean, veterans back from the same war with a theological basis quite similar to that of the worker priests began a different type of experiment in Christian ministry. They went into one of America's worst slums, East Harlem in New York City. Street gangs, dope peddlers, rent-gougers and corrupt politicians ruled the area. Exactly in the midst of this misery did the war veterans set up their parish in the belief that a close-knit Christian community might learn to meet the district's staggering social and spiritual needs.

Sister parishes grew up in a dozen or so cities across the United States. In Chicago it was called the West Side Christian Parish. In 1957 I joined the Chicago parish and was assigned as a pastor to a small storefront church. My congregation was black and my parish was a slum area of south Chicago. The physical, social and spiritual misery of the people was lived out in their daily lives of unemployment, poverty and indignity. They were victims of a white system that was not far removed from slavery.

Despite the misery, however, there was an astonishing faith that God would save. For my parishioners there was no artificial separation between salvation in the next world and salvation in this. No sophisticated division between personal salvation and social justice. Their faith included it all. Salvation applied across the board. Their eyes were on the "Promised Land" across the River Jordan, but also on the land of "Chicago" where God called for better housing, more jobs and quality education.

The worker priests, the East Harlem Protestant Parish, and the West Side Christian Parish were part of the inheritance that I carried with me as I crossed the Pacific Ocean and began a missionary's life in Inchun, Korea. I did not know the word *han* at that time, but in looking back I realize that the *han* of the French workers and my black parishioners in Chicago had shaped much of my emerging theology.

Once in Korea I found myself among a wonderful conglomeration of people called missionaries. They were of every size, shape, form and persuasion. With several I disagreed about lifestyle and theology, but gradually I came to have respect for most of them and deep affection for many. I came to realize that I was within a great crowd of people whose witnesses dated back a hundred years. Ester Laird was one of my contemporaries. She was a frail woman with Parkinson's disease who daily visited the refugees who, in 1954, lived in the river bed in Taejon. She cared for the sick and carried their undernourished babies on her own back. Before her was Victor Peters whom I never met, but about whom I heard many stories. Victor gave up Western living, Western clothes and Western food so that his "foreignness" would not be an obstacle to the gospel. Before him was Frank Williams, an energetic and dedicated man who for twenty years walked over mountains and into remote villages of Choong-chung Nam-do Province preaching, teaching and gathering congregations.

And within the drama and heroics of the March 1, 1919 Independence Movement is hidden the missionary Frank Scofield. Prior to him was the legendary James Gale who knew that the Christian gospel had to be communicated while sitting cross-legged on the floor in the humble homes of common people, and John Nevius whose advice in 1893 led the Council of Missions, an interdenominational missionary organization, to declare that: "1) It is better to aim at the conversion of the working classes than that of the higher classes; 2) the conversion of women and the education of Christian girls shall be given serious consideration; and 3) it is better to translate and publish the Bible and Christian literature in 'Hangul,' the vernacular language of the minjung, rather than in Chinese characters."[3]

I would like to think that my missionary witness was done in the same spirit as these brothers and sisters, and the many others whom they represent.

Inchun UIM

At the 1961 Annual Conference of the Korean Methodist church, Bishop Kim Chong-pil appointed me to Urban Industrial Mission in the city of Inchun. There I met three Korean people with concerns similar to mine, and whose subsequent lives were to have a deep effect upon my own.

All three were Methodist pastors, and all three agreed that

the gospel required us to overcome the great gulf that existed between the church and working class. We were convinced that regular church ministries and revival meetings would not meet the need. We decided to join the work force. More accurately, we decided that Cho Sung-hyuk, Cho Moon-gul and Cho Wha-soon (the three Cho's) would find employment in Inchun's factories. As a foreigner, I did not seek employment, but rather addressed myself to the labor unions of the city.

Why did we decide to leave the regular channels and move into areas where we were all foreigners? We were all convinced that the evangelical task of the church in regard to industrial workers was not being done. The gulf was too wide. We were not clear, however, in our own minds as to what the evangelical task really was. We were praying that the answer to this question would be revealed to us as we ventured into the world of the worker. In other words, we were of a faith that through the minjung of the factories and unions, we would discover something new about Jesus and his call to discipleship. We were hoping that God would, through the daily lives of industrial workers, reveal something to us about Jesus that we did not yet know. We located ourselves among the minjung expective revelation so that God could use us to be evangelists in their midst.

We did not know what we were asking. The revelations came, but they came in shapes different from any we expected and they brought a mandate that we did not seek.

Revelations

Though our entrance into the world of labor was looked at as novel or even radical, we were, in fact, groping in the dark. We were very conventional with regard to the expression of our theology and our attempts to get workers to come out to church. The more we got involved, however, the more we were challenged by the workers to rethink and reformulate our own understanding of God.

One of the first of the revelations came to Cho Moon-gul. He worked for five years in a steel mill, handling the red hot bars of metal as they came hissing out of the pressing machine. One day he lost the rhythm of his motion and stepped back onto a molten bar of steel. His shoe was burned off and his ankle suffered deep wounds. For weeks he could hardly walk. He suffered tremendously and felt like a martyr. To his surprise and chagrin, however, he got little sympathy from his fellow workers. He may have been a martyr in his mind, but not in theirs. After the pain subsided and Moon-gul could forget himself a bit, he began to piece together his experience. Accidents, injuries and even death were such a common part of the steel workers' lives that Moon-gul's wounds seemed to be nothing. To Moon-gul, and the rest of us, this came not as cold, objective fact (though it was that also), but as a revelatory look into the *han* of the workers.

Cho Sung-hyuk's insight came by a different route. He worked in a plywood factory. One afternoon he was assigned to help un-load trucks full of 4-ply plywood sheets. He and three other men caught the wood as it was unloaded by two men on top of the truck. The two unloaders began to make sport of the men below. They would drop the wood when they did not expect it or throw it down with force. An argument arose and things got heated. Fi-nally in desperation Sung-hyuk yelled, "Do that one more time and I'll come up there and knock the shit out of you!" The anger of his voice or the look of his eyes must have been persuasive for the men on the truck backed off and unloaded the wood as they were supposed to.

At the instant he challenged the two men to a fight, Reverend Cho was made aware of a fact of life that was as obvious as the air he breathed, but yet had never reached his level of conscious-ness: The people he worked among were always being dumped on by some tyrants like the truck men, or the supervisors or the plant managers. Being oppressed was their existence, their fate. Theirs truly was the *han* spoken of years later by minjung theology.

Reverend Cho Wha-soon's eye-opener came the very first day on the job. After she was made to wait for two hours, the supervis-or finally came out of his office. In sharp, unfriendly terms he commanded her to report to the kitchen detail. When she walked in the door, a middle-aged matron snapped, "Where the hell have you been. Get those tables cleaned off and the floor scrubbed." The attitude was hostile and the words demeaning. Af-ter a few hours of such treatment Reverend Cho had had it. She was ready to explode in anger and frustration.

She was about to let the older woman have both barrels and walk out when a voice of another sort caught her attention. That voice was one that welled up within her and said, "This is the way that Christ was treated. Are you better than he?"

Cho Wha-soon finished scrubbing the floor and became a textile worker.

The final story of our introduction to *han* relates to a visit I made to the Dock Workers' Union in 1964.

The office was a small hut next to the wharf. The men carried much of the ship's cargo on their own shoulders and back by walking very gingerly down planks that led from ship to shore. I walked into the union office and immediately saw Mr. Song, a good Presbyterian layman. As we talked, other men came in. They had just finished a job. They were curious about a foreigner being among them, but not at all bashful, and soon we were talking about everything from religion to their chronic backaches caused by the heavy work. In the midst of the conversation a call came from dockside, "All out! Let's work!" Instantly they were on their feet and out the door. And in that instant a new discovery snapped into my brain, "Jesus and his disciples were probably something like these coarse, hard-working men. The fishermen of Galilee and the carpenter of Nazareth."

Each of the four of us experienced our own introduction to the *han* of the workers. Each shared that experience with the others. All of us identified the *han* as a means of revelation to us. Jesus once more walked and suffered among us. The incarnation was again observed. The teachings of the gospel became a personal and social reality.

Han and Jesus

The acceptance of *han* as revelatory, however, raises two questions: 1) What is the relationship between the actions of God in Christ as they were played out in Palestine so long ago and the industrial workers of twentieth century Korea, most of whom know nothing about Jesus of Nazareth? And 2) Is *han* revelatory for those who are doing the suffering? Is it not "our" interpretation of "their" suffering which gives it meaning to us? If so, where does that leave the minjung who do not share that interpretation?

The first question is as old as the Christian movement itself. Are Jesus and the Kingdom the fulfillment of the Old Testament or does Jesus usher in a new age discontinuous with the past? Did the gospel shed light upon and complete the unknown gods of ancient Greece or was it a complete scandal to non-Christians? The same either/or question confronted the early Jesuits in China: Does

Christianity fulfill Confucianism or are the two antithetical? And the worker priests of France were asking the same question in regard to the working class of a supposedly Christian nation.

Among missionaries in the twentieth century, the debate has waxed heavy. In 1932 William E. Hocking declared that he recognized a common foundation among all religions and the missionary enterprise should focus on comparing Christian teachings with those of others so that the religions and peoples of the world could enrich one another. Henrick Kraemer retorted that though there were noble things in all religions, only the Christian religion was a revealed religion. The others were of human creation. Christ, he claimed, was discontinuous with all religions, coming to them from the outside.

The revelations and experiences received over two decades among Korea's industrial workers teach that both Hocking and Kraemer are, to some degree, correct. There most certainly is a commonality that binds all humanity together. Hocking had a point when he advised the Western missionary to resist feeling that he or she had the superior religion. Hocking advised them to listen and learn for God is revealed also in the pagan.

A Common Humanity

The industrial workers of Korea are of many religions and no religion. Yet there is that common humanity, common decency, common spiritual aspirations, and common evil that makes us all brothers and sisters. There is also the "sameness" of spiritual and physical suffering that has been the context for the poor for all ages.

There is in Scripture a depiction of social-economic structures that continually perpetuate the oppression of the poor; structures against which Yahweh God's word of justice is always directed. Leviticus 25 and Deuteronomy 15 portray an economic system in which ownership of land, livestock and food was heavily concentrated in the hands of a few. Workers were often enslaved and never paid above a subsistence wage. Indebtedness to the money lenders was staggering and the impoverished roamed the land.

This class system of a few rich and masses of poor seems to have extended throughout the existence of Israel. It is this system, these structures of concentration of ownership, indebtedness of the citizens, exploitation of labor against which Yahweh God inveighs. In Leviticus and Deuteronomy Yahweh's demands are clear. They address the economic and social structures head on: 1) break up the large land holdings and give the land to the landless; 2) free the enslaved workers; 3) establish means whereby the poor can provide for themselves; and 4) write off the indebtedness of the people. Then Yahweh supplies the value base for the new society. Remember once you were all slaves in Egypt, but now you are all brothers and sisters in your own land. The land and all in it is for your common good. Secondly, Yahweh says: "The poor you will always have with you; therefore do not close your hand nor your mind against them. Rather, always reform your structures so that they can be integrated into the productive system."

A similar system of social stratification can be found in Korean society in the twentieth century. The great Confucian teacher, Mencius, once said there are two types of people: the ruler and the ruled. The Japanese rulers from 1910-1945 certainly agreed with Mencius, and though much has been said about democracy and freedom in South Korea since 1945, the rulers of Korean society have been very reluctant to permit their exercise. Owners of Korean industry still insist on the ancient paternalism of deference and obedience on the part of employees. Unions are never accepted and individuals who attempt collective action are dismissed. And, since 1970, military dictators have forbade citizen participation in government. All of these modern versions of the ruler and ruled are practiced in the name of a new religion, "anti-communism."

William Hocking points to the commonality of humanity and spirituality that bind one people to all others. He could have gone further and pointed to the persistence of socioeconomic structures that have divided societies in the two classes of ruler and ruled. He could have noticed how Jesus had his own identity among those who were called the people and the sinners. Jesus' being in solidarity with the minjung of his day put him in solidarity also with the minjung of South Korea.

The people, the parables, the miracles, and the cross of Jesus are all square with the class stratified society of industrialized Korea. Revelations received through the *han* of the workers seem to make the transfer of Jesus from old Israel to modern Korea quite easy and natural. We find ourselves agreeing with the Brazilian theologian, Leonardo Boff, when he refers to theology emerging from non-Christians, directed toward non-Christians and performed with non-Christians.

The Evangel

It cannot, however, be claimed that in some mysterious fashion Korean workers were able to sense instinctively the presence of Christ among them—even though the person of Jesus does seem to have an appeal to some workers who are not Christian. I remember sitting one night in a wine house with some steel workers and to my surprise the conversation came around to Jesus' crucifixion. "Wasn't Jesus killed because he was one of the people?" "He was killed by the same powers that are on our back." "His sufferings were a lot like ours." These remarks made by non-church people indicate an insight into the experience of forced suffering common to them and Jesus.

Be that as it may, it does not answer the question of whether *han* is revelatory to the minjung. I do not believe that we can claim that suffering and outrage in and of themselves open eyes to God or heaven. Nor do they provide hope. They may beget anger, hate or despair, and these emotions may be necessary if the minjung are to liberate themselves from bondage. But in and of itself, *han* and the emotions related thereto are not sufficient to produce personal or social salvation. *Han* may erupt in revolt or momentary protest, but if that eruption is to be sustained to bring about reform (personal and social) some sympathetic power from the outside is needed; some faith that promises hope for the future must be present. Henrick Kraemer's argument in the debate mentioned above speaks to this point.

Kraemer is right in his assertion that Jesus is discontinuous with all religions (including Christianity) and all human societies. He is the new dimension that has come into history. Through him humanity and social structures have an opportunity to clearly view the love and justice of God. He is revelation from the outside. But he becomes revelation to us only as he is in solidarity with the sufferings of the poor; he challenged the principalities and powers that oppress people and would not back down; he became God because he was resurrected over the power of the principalities.

Kraemer's claim for the uniqueness for Christ is pertinent, but it is that very uniqueness that transports Christ down through the ages in solidarity, in incarnation, with the sufferings of the poor, the *han* of the minjung.

This solidarity and otherness of Jesus sets the dialectical pat-

tern within which his disciples move. On the one hand the minjung mediate Jesus to the disciples and open to them a community
of brothers and sisters. At the same time the disciple recognizes
the other side of the dialectic: He is an evangelist of Jesus who
provides meaning and salvation from outside humanity. As the
word "incarnation" indicates, commonality and evangelism are
held together in "creative tension" by the disciples that *see*
Christ through the minjung. Evangelism and commonality are always within the context of receiving grace and accepting kinship.

The dialectical position places the disciples in conflict with
the religious and political establishment just as it did in the case
of Jesus. Conflict is unavoidable. The important thing is whether
the conflict arises because the gospel is being rightly declared;
that is, whether or not the conflict comes as a result of Christian
evangelists standing with the poor against violations of their
Kingdom-given dignity as brothers and sisters of Christ. Here is
where community is created and here is where the power of the
Kingdom is made visible for all to see.

Han Powerlessness

Leonardo Boff, a Brazilian priest, and Kim Chi Ha, a layman,
speak of ugliness. The dominant milieu of the poor is ugliness, an
ugliness of surroundings and of human relations, that frequently
becomes internalized into their very persons. The people and their
society suffer both the *han* of physical oppression and spiritual
debasement. *Han* may be defined as having an eruptive anger, a
potential for revolt, but if it is defined that way, then we must
coin another term that is "pre-*han*," or "sub-*han*." The ugliness under which many live and the crushing blows that many sustain
kills the spirit and strangles the breath of protest. Let us not be romantic about the senseless suffering inflicted upon the minjung and
the poor all over the world.

In the case of the Peoples' Revolutionary Party (PRP) eight innocent men were hanged and their families stigmatized forever as
"communists." This suffering had no reason other than that military men needed a scapegoat in order to justify their tyranny. There
may also have been a bit of a personal vendetta on the part of the
chief prosecutor. The accused never had a chance. At the moment
the KCIA (Korean CIA) decided to take them in they were as good
as dead. They were tortured, made to confess, paraded through a

charade of court appeals and then hanged in loneliness behind prison walls. They suffered perhaps even more than Jesus did. Yet, there is no story of resurrection for them or their families.

A similar fate was the reward of the staff of Urban Industrial Mission (UIM). After Park Chong-hee and his KCIA took control of Korean society in 1971, UIM members became hounded members of society. Lay people were intimidated and threatened with the loss of jobs. Reverend Cho Wha-soon disappeared for three months. Released by the KCIA and then shortly thereafter again imprisoned for over a year, Cho Sung-hyuk was beaten and his life threatened. Other UIM people and sympathizers were treated just as harshly. I underwent interrogation on five different occasions. Probably because I was an American, I was deported rather than imprisoned or tortured.

All of this violence against us was justified in the name of "anti-communism." Even the institutional churches pull back when one is marked by the sign of the beast called "communist." The revelations received through the *han* of the workers led only to more sufferings. The principalities and powers control the day.

But when speaking of *han* one must also name the oppressor. Was it not Kim Chi Ha's poem, "The Five Bandits," that first got him into trouble with the authorities? Was it not because Jesus identified the scribes and Pharisees, the rich and the powerful, as the inflictors of unjust suffering that he was crucified? If one is to take *han* seriously, then the cause of that condition must be clearly identified and opposed. The pattern of Deuteronomy 15 is an appropriate one to follow. Yahweh explicitly enumerates the oppressor's various shapes and then supplies explicit remedies for each. In today's world of transnational corporations and international military alignment, it is often hard to identify the actual source of oppression. People, not all of them economically poor, become pawns, alienated and powerless, participating in a *han* that once was reserved for the poor. The principalities and powers still hold the upper hand and attempt to remain anonymous. If the debilitating dimension of *han* is to be overcome, the exploiters must be named and held to public view.

Han Power

To say that the minjung are powerless and at the mercy of the principalities and powers of this world does not, however, deny that there is that *han* that has incubating within it the power for revolt. Unfortunately, revolt or protest is not sufficient. It can be snuffed out or its leaders co-opted into the dominating system.

The *han* which carries the seed of involvement must be organized if it is to be efficacious for the establishment of justice. Labor unions, community organizations, political parties of the poor, and mutual development groups are essential. The military rulers of Korea, or elsewhere, know this instinctively. That is why they very quickly eradicate unions and other organizations of the people. Those who espouse minjung theology also realize this organizational dimension of *han* and it is at that juncture that they come into conflict with the authorities. If they could confine their theology to isolated efforts of individuals they would have little trouble with the government.

Indeed it is because the *han* experience is collective that it demands organization. The female workers in South Korea's factories demonstrate this collective pattern. Though they have been beaten on every occasion, it is their persistence that keeps the spirit of the labor movement alive. Unions are in captivity to the military, but again and again the *han* of women has exploded and kept the names of the oppressor before the public view.

The case of Tong Il Bangjik is instructive. When Reverend Cho Wha-soon entered Tong Il as a laborer, the young women, recently from the countryside, were alienated from one another and demoralized because of the harsh treatment received at the hands of factory supervisors. Gradually Reverend Cho gathered the women together to share one another's hardship. They found a place outside the factory to talk and be family. They came to cry together and learned to laugh together. They developed confidence and trust in one another, and with the assistance of Reverend Cho they learned how to organize.

Then the unexpected happened: The women of Tong Il Bangjik voted in a woman as president of their labor union. Previously the union had been controlled by a company-backed male worker. The women took over and, to the surprise of management, administered the union with skill and unheard-of energy. The *han* that had smoldered within them gave birth to a collective expression of freedom and new humanity. The company, however, could not cope with the new situation. They could not accept women as equals and they would not negotiate such serious matters as wages and working conditions with "girls."

The Tong Il Bangjik union was destroyed. The company and the military rulers cried violence. The women, most of whom were teenagers, were, the company charged, threatening people, obstructing economic development and causing social disorder. To stop the "violence" of the young women, the company hired a cadre of goons to beat them up and throw them out. "Violence" is often charged by the authorities when the minjung attempt to organize for self-protection and self-expression. Any objective analysis would witness to the violence of the Korean military regime and the corporations that help maintain it, but it is the minjung organizing to prevent violence against themselves whom the regime labels as violent communists. The example set by the Tong Il Bangjik women has been repeated time and again over the last decade by other young women in a dozen factories throughout Korea. If *han* is a "starting point for a new human history" as Moon Dong-whan claims, then it must be organized. Young female industrial workers have kept one option of organization alive for all to see—and marvel.

Conversion, Conflict, and the Institutional Church

The institutional church will never be converted to minjung theology. It is too much integrated into the values and institutions of capitalism to ever become minjung. Paradoxically neither can it expel minjung theology from itself. The correlations between minjung and the Bible are too close and too obvious for the church to completely expunge it. There will always be Christians and non-Christians who will point out this affinity between Christ and the poor and as such they will be a judgment on the church, a challenge. Minjung theology speaks of *dan*, or a break with the past, repentance plus a turning toward justice. Because of the presence of minjung theology within its body, the church is confronted with the opportunity of *dan*. Some will hear and move toward justice. Some will begin to live into the Kingdom. They will be the ones who will be converted to the evangelical task of solidarity with the minjung through Jesus of Nazareth.

The committed presence of those who go through *dan* not only provides a repentance-witness to the church. Ironically the "*dan*-faction" appropriates, at least to some extent, the social-religious authority of the church. Because the "*dan*-people" are within the body of the conventional church, their voice is heard not as the voice of a small number of individuals, but as a voice of the church. Thus the witness, humble and weak though it is, often exerts a strength beyond itself. Society, hearing the witness, is disturbed because it is being put under judgment by what it mistakenly perceives of as the church. Yet the minjung are a voice that bears witness to the church, to what the church should be—a church passed through *dan* and alive for justice.

The principalities and powers of society often perceive this voice as a church-empowered threat to progressive control of society, and they become frantic. The brutal repression of groups perceived by the government as church-affiliated demonstrates this point.

Will society and its authorities receive the witness and repent? Not likely! It is almost inconceivable for a ruler in government or business to say, "I have sinned. Forgive me." And, it is beyond expectation that a corporation might openly and honestly repent of wrong-doing against its workers. Corporations and rules do, however, react and sometimes change. Defensive reaction comes even when weak voices are raised. Change comes, however, only as an inescapable reflex to sustained and organized power. A collective expression of *han*, as demonstrated by the women of Tong Il Bangjik, might bring change if it can be sustained and widened.

To a large extent the results of the "*dan*-people's" witness cannot be predicted. The consequences in terms of oppression can often be foreseen, but the results in the form of conversion and the establishment of justice are elusive. Nevertheless, the urgency of the call remains: Repent, for the Kingdom of God is among you!

Notes

1. Minjung is a Korean word defined by Moon Dong-whan as all those people who are politically, economically, socially and culturally oppressed and alienated by the existing system of society. *Korean-American Relations at Crossroads*, ed. Wonmo Dong (Princeton, N.J.: The Association of Korean Christian Scholars in North America, Inc., 1982), p. 17.

2. *Han* is defined by the poet, Kim Chi Ha, as the minjung's angry and sad sentiment turned inward, hardened, and stuck to their hearts. *Han* is caused as one's "outgoing-ness" is blocked and pressed for an extended period of time by external oppression and exploitation, p. 17.

3. Quoted from *Fire beneath the Frost*, ed. Peggy Billings (New York: Friendship Press, 1984).

The Story of Paligonju
(From legend)

In the early days there was a king who had no son, only daughters. When the seventh daughter was born, he was greatly angered at her and put her in a stone box and cast it into a pond. Heaven, however, extended mercy and sent a dragon king to rescue the girl from the pond and to bring her to heaven. This daughter, Paligonju, lived happily in the heavenly palace.

One day her father, because of his sinful act, became critically ill. Her mother heard that the only thing that could cure his illness was the medicine water in the western sky. Her mother asked the other six daughters, who grew up in their father's home, to go to the place of the western sky. But all of them declined to go to the western sky for it was too difficult a place to reach.

It was Paligonju, the rejected princess, who volunteered to go to the western sky and get the medicine water. She was only 14 years old when she descended to the earth to see her ailing father. When she arrived at the western sky after various hardships and troubles, the well-keeper asked for some money in return for the medicine water. But Paligonju did not have any money. Therefore she had to work three years gathering firewood, three years cooking, and another three years drawing water from the well. In spite of all these years of hard labor, the keeper still did not allow her to take the water back to her father. Finally, she had to marry him and gave birth to seven sons. Finally she was given permission to take the medicine water home to her father. When she came back to earth, her father and her mother were dead. The medicine water she brought from the western sky was able to revive them and restore them to health. As a result, she became the champion of rejected and oppressed women in Korea.

Minjung Theology
in Women's Perspective
by Letty M. Russell

If three women get together, a plate will be broken.[1]

For centuries Korean women have been taught that their very being is trivial and inferior—even talking together will come to no good and is not considered productive. Against this background Korean women and other women from Asia are beginning to join in articulating their own human dignity and the gifts they can bring to theological action and reflection. As C.S. Song has put it in *Third Eye Theology*, "The Women's Liberation Movement is an effort on the part of women to fulfill their spirituality. As long as they have to submit to men, as long as social conventions require them to suppress their talents and longing, their spirituality is incarcerated. They are not free to create."[2]

I am deeply impressed by the actions and the writings of minjung theologians, and am honored to be invited to respond to the book, *Minjung Theology: People as the Subjects of History*. This book's articulation of a Korean theology that emerges out of a unique socioeconomic and cultural history, and a deep commitment to political struggle for justice in Korea, is a great contribution to the field of liberation/feminist theologies.[3] As a white, middle-class woman, living in the United States, I participate in the structures of oppression that bring despair and death to the very subjects of minjung theology. Yet I strive in my work to be part of the solution and not just the problem, and I welcome this opportunity to continue the dialogue with my Korean sisters and brothers. I only regret that I am limited to the very small part of that conversation that is available in English.

In this response I try to stand in solidarity with the minjung theologians as I listen and learn from their work. I also seek to reflect critically on minjung theology from a feminist perspective by sharing points of convergence and difference that I consider important in the development of both minjung and feminist theologies.

Lastly, I attempt to highlight the ongoing concerns and work of Asian and Korean women theologians. They were largely missing partners in the dialogue at the time of the discussion and publication (1979-83) of *Minjung Theology*.

Discovering Third World Women's Theologies

In discussing the development of Third World Women's theologies, it is important to bear in mind that these theologies are not just being developed, they are being discovered![4] That is, Third World women and Asian women are discovering their voices, their stories and their commitment to their own people as rich resources for the articulation of theology in each context. Much of their heritage is formed already in theologies of story, song and tradition. They are each sharing stories that illuminate the concrete life situation of their people, yet also cross cultures, speak of common humanity.

Roots of My Commitment

My own commitment to the liberation of the oppressed is rooted in a long story, and connected to the society and culture of the USA. The roots were formed through a ministry shared with the people of the East Harlem Protestant Parish in New York City where I served as an educator and pastor for 17 years. By the time I left East Harlem in 1969 to begin teaching in seminary, people had taught me a great deal about the meaning of exodus and resurrection in a situation of poverty, racism, and sexism where the black and hispanic residents lived without hope. At the same time I was discovering a great deal about the world church. Through the work of the World Council of Churches and the World YWCA, I was learning about the need for indigenous structures in the life of the churches as they sought to incarnate the gospel message in each place.

My first trip to Asia was with my husband, Hans Hoekendijk, who was Professor of Missions at Union Theological Seminary in New York. We taught together for one term at the United Theological College in Bangalore, India, and I also worked as a part-time religious consultant for the YWCA of India. We then visited other Asian countries, including Indonesia, where my husband was born and raised. Although this trip did not take me to Korea, it did prepare me for my increasing discovery of women doing theol-

ogy around the world, and my work as an advocate for the participation of women in the World Council of Churches at the Nairobi
Assembly and in the following years.

My most recent visit to Asia was in 1983. I visited Japan and Korea at the invitation of Aiko Carter, Secretary of the Women's Committee of the National Christian Council of Japan, and of Chung
Sook-ja, Secretary for the Korean Association of Women Theologians. I had been asked to lecture on feminist theology by women
who were already struggling to discover the meaning of their own
theology as women. In a sense, the women discovered me as a re-
source for their work, and in turn gave me a brief opportunity to sit
with them in their own contexts. In Korea I re-discovered firsthand
what it meant to struggle for human rights and how minjung theology was hammered out week by week in that context. From my perspective as a feminist, I was most excited to discover the beginning of
feminist minjung theology among the theologically trained women.

The Agenda of Asian Women Theologians

Korean women theologians are playing an important role in the
discovery of Asian women's theologies because of their unique situation. With about 30 percent of Korea's population being Christian, they have many more resources to draw upon in their church
women's organizations and educational institutions. At the same
time the political situation of Korea has conscienticized women
along with men in the struggles of democracy and justice. This
same situation is also causing an increasing number of Korean wom-
en to live and study in other countries where they join in building
networks of support with other Asian women.

One of these networks in the USA is the group called Asian
Women Theologians (AWT). This group is committed both to building networks of support that can continue when they return to Asia,
and to working with one another in the development of women's
theologies in their own nations. Their work in the USA is providing new links among Asian feminists and Asian American feminists,
as well as with women of all colors in the USA. Speaking at a
meeting of Asian Women Theologians, Southern California, Kwok
Pui Lan of Hong Kong underlined their present task:

Asian feminist theology has to fight a battle on two fronts.
On the one hand, we have to unmask the patriarchal ele-

ments in our cultures; on the other, we have to engage ourselves in serious critique of the patriarchal tradition of
Christianity....Secondly, we have to retrieve our past traditions which have liberated and empowered women....This
leads to the final step of a construction of Asian feminist theology which is both Asian and Christian. The theology must
be able to address the present oppression of Asian women, to
articulate the power and hope of women as subjects of our own
destiny, and to empower women in our long road to freedom.[5]

Another network is being created through a series of national, regional, and international meetings of women in Third World theology sponsored by the Ecumenical Association of Third World
Theologians (EATWOT). According to the theme of the Asian conference held in November 1985 in the Philippines, their agenda is
nothing less than *Total Liberation*.[6] The model for their reflection, as seen in the Korean preparatory meeting of KAWT, was to
begin with the stories of the oppressed (laborer, farmer, urban
poor) and then to proceed to sociocritical analysis and theological
reflection on the meaning of these concrete stories of oppression.
The links to minjung theology are becoming ever clearer. Representatives of KAWT subsequently met with the minjung theologians
under the sponsorship of the Korean Centre for Theological Studies. Under the leadership of Lee Oo-chung as President and Ahn
Sang-nim as Secretary, KAWT has begun direct involvement in
the struggle of the women factory workers. The KAWT women
also joined 13 other Korean women's organizations in a "Declaration of the Women's Movement in 1985—Together with the Nation, Democracy and the People's Movement" on the eve of International Women's Day.[7]

As Reverend Park Sun-ai, poet and editor of *In God's Image*,
has put it, the agenda of the women's movement in Asia is to
spread a movement of new life.

> A stone is thrown
> into a calm lake
> and the stone made waves
> spreading, reaching to the far end
>
> Till the whole lake
> starts bubbling with life

Till the whole lake
makes its own spring
to keep its own life going
23 April 1985[8]

Minjung and Feminist Theologies in Dialogue

At first glance one might assume that there is very little for a
white, U.S. feminist theologian and minjung theologians about
which to dialogue. One could hardly expect U.S. feminists to be
welcomed with open arms by those who struggle daily to overcome
not only the results of U.S. economic and military exploitation, but
also a history of First World domination in church life and theological reflection. Yet this is not the beginning point of such a dialogue. We begin together in our common task of opposition to the
sources of oppression which we find both within and outside of
ourselves. One of the major sources of such oppression is the sin of
sexism, a universal system of marginalization of women that im-
poses double oppression on those already oppressed by poverty,
race and class in both First and Third Worlds. Feminist and minjung theologians have in common their recognition that, in spite of
personal reluctance and fear, it is impossible to do adequate social
or theological analysis without including sexism as part of the in-
terlocking web of oppression and death which dominates our divided world (*Minjung Theology*, p. 35).

A second point for dialogue can be found in the way in which
both the critical analysis and theological method used by the
minjung and feminist theologians cross over geographical boundaries so that they share parallel agendas with each other and
with other Third World theologies. For instance, the strong emphasis on historical and cultural analysis and the use of Asian
religious traditions is paralleled by the work U.S. feminists are
doing on non-Christian and post-Christian religions.

The most important common link between feminist theologians
of all colors and worlds with liberation theologians of all colors
and worlds is their beginning point of commitment to the liberation of the oppressed. But it is not just the commitment to act and
the inductive starting point in the stories of struggle that forges
the links in the freedom chain. For when we act in solidarity with
the oppressed we discover our own marginalization and rejection.

At this *point of pain* we begin to be able to theologize in solidarity with others who suffer in our midst and around the world.[9]

Speaking out of my own experiences of struggle I do not wish to universalize my perspective, but rather to point out three themes from minjung theology which have echoes in the stories of women in the USA and Korea as they work to discover themselves as subjects of their own theologies. Among the many rich and fascinating possibilities I have chosen to discuss are: the subject of theology, authority of experience, and messianic politics.

The Subject of Theology

Although the minjung are the subject of minjung theology, there has been "...a certain resistance to defining or conceptualizing the term" (*Minjung Theology*, p. 42). According to Suh Kwang-sun David, this is because the Korean term comes from a very rich history of struggle among the Korean people and is not reducible simply to the proletariat or economically oppressed. In addition, such a scientific definition would objectify the minjung and make them an object of study rather than those who are the subjects of theology. Minjung is "...a living reality which is dynamic and changing, and it has to define itself as subject" (*Minjung Theology*, pp. 34, 184-185). It does this through its own social, political and cultural biography learned through the recovery of history, as well as through sharing in the current struggles of the minjung against oppression.

The *ochlos* of the Bible are seen in Mark to be those whom Jesus loved: the sinners, tax collectors, sick, those opposed to the powers in Jerusalem, the despised people of Galilee, prostitutes, etc. (Mark 2:13-17). In the same way the minjung are those who are "...politically oppressed, economically exploited, socially marginalized and culturally despised and ignored" (*Minjung Theology*, pp. 35, 142-143).[10] They include a variety of overlapping categories of those who have shared in the deep, unresolved suffering of the Korean people. In his chapter, "Towards a Theology of *Han*," Suh Nam-dong speaks of the nation as a whole suffering repeated invasions; the majority of Korean people who are *han*-ridden and suffering exploitation from their rulers; women who suffer under Confucian patriarchy; and slaves who at one time numbered about half of the population (*Minjung Theology*, p. 58).

But there are problems with speaking of the minjung as the subject of theology. The first is that only some academically trained theologians are qualified to speak as subjects whose words are *of* and *by* the minjung, not just *about* them. They join the minjung as part of an oppressed people and nation (but not as slaves or women). In categories where they do not fit as subjects, the theologians reflect on the stories of others and work through cultural biography. The biography of the writers themselves who have discovered the minjung through their own sufferings in the political struggle for justice establishes yet another major link to the minjung experience. "Theology of minjung is a sociopolitical biography of Korean Christians" (*Minjung Theology*, p. 16).

A second problem (or opportunity) is that the stress on the minjung as the subject of theology forces a refocusing of theology itself. In what sense does it continue to be thinking about *God* as God is known in and through the lives of the minjung? It would seem that the story of the minjung can function as a paradigm or metaphor for God's dealing with humanity. Yet in some places in *Minjung Theology* the stress is clearly the other way, with the story of Jesus clarifying the messianic role of the minjung. Thus Suh Nam-dong says that Jesus is not the subject matter of minjung theology: "In the case of minjung theology, Jesus is the means for understanding the minjung correctly, rather than the concept of 'minjung' being the instrument for understanding Jesus (160)."

In the same way, he attributes a uniqueness to the minjung that makes it impossible to translate, even with the term *ochlos* which only partly clarifies its meaning (*Minjung Theology*, pp. 142-152, 160). In my perspective such a position could lead to a romanticization of the minjung. Their importance as a living reality in the Korean context makes their evolving story a privileged, but not an exclusive, source of truth about God. This question about the authority of experience in Christian theology needs to be explored further after we look at some of the parallels between the descriptions of "minjung" and "feminist."

It is interesting that feminist theologians have also had endless discussions about how to name what they are about. Especially because the name "feminist" has a negative connotation among many church women and among many people in the Third World, it has continued to be a stumbling block in the dialogue about our common task. In fact, on my trip to Asia one of the major questions put to me repeatedly was whether it is possible to be a Christian and a feminist. Like the word "communist" in the U.S. and South

Korea, the word "feminist" often evokes an instant reaction of "ungodly radical" and "threat to family and society." For a long time many of us did not use the word, as we were more concerned to reach out to other women than to claim a particular term. But in clarifying what we were about, it became clear that the naming of our task was important to the task itself.

Just as the minjung theologians have chosen a description that cuts across categories of class to clarify their role as participants in the theology, feminist theologians have chosen the word feminist because it can indicate any person (male or female) who is an advocate of the equality of women and men of every race, class, and nationality. This does not eliminate the epistemological privilege of women, especially women from the underside of society, in the formation of feminist theology, for they are the ones who must say what equality and freedom will mean. But it does reach out beyond a small group of white, middle class, females in the first World.

This commitment of those who call themselves feminist is underlined and defined by Barbara Smith in an article on racism and women's studies: "Feminism is the political theory and practice that struggles to free *all* women: women of color, working-class women, poor women, disabled women, lesbians, old women—as well as white, economically privileged, heterosexual women. Anything less than this vision of total freedom is not feminism, but merely female self-aggrandizement."[11] Feminist theologies seek to act and reflect upon this search for liberation from all forms of dehumanization as those who join God in advocating full human dignity of each and every person.

Unlike other contextual theologies, such as minjung and black theology, feminist theology is not limited to one particular racial or national group. In order to clarify its content it must always add a second word to the name. Feminist theologies as such are never just feminist. They are white feminist, minjung feminist, black feminist, and the like. But the word "feminist" is a political word and indicates the style of advocacy and commitment that is characteristic of liberation theologies. The word "feminist" cannot be assumed in a particular liberation theology because the structures of patriarchy are still operating within that framework to make women the objects and not the co-subjects of theology. Feminism advocates the full humanity of women who face oppression from the social structures of patriarchy in its many different cultural forms. Elisabeth Schüssler Fiorenza has characterized this manifestation of the principalities and powers in this way: "*Patriarchy* as a male pyramid of graded subordinations and exploitations specifies women's oppression in terms of the class, race, country, or religion of the men to whom we 'belong.'"[12]

The debate over whether woman or God is the subject of theology is also very much part of the picture in the United States. But the word "feminist" allows the possibility of God being the subject, while the perspective is one of advocacy for the full humanity of women. The issue of God as subject becomes very complex for feminists because of the identification of God with patriarchal social, economic, political and ecclesial thought patterns of domination. The god who has reinforced the status quo through the religion of the rulers is still alive and well in every part of the Christian church as the Father who insures the ontological necessity of women's subordination to the male representatives of God. For this reason feminists also find themselves appealing to the authority of their own experience as they wrestle with biblical and church tradition. As Mary Ann Tolbert has put it: "...one must struggle against God as enemy assisted by God as helper, or one must defeat the Bible as patriarchal authority by using the Bible as liberator."[13]

In Korea, women are also caught up in these patriarchal structures. Even women theologians find themselves assigned a status in terms of their husband and family, and thus constantly live the double message of liberation and subordination. The Christian gospel says they are to be free of the cultural stereotypes of male and female, but at the same time biblical interpretation reinforces the Confucian idea of order through subordination. There is to be harmony in the home through complementarity, yet this harmony is to be preserved at the expense of the one who has the least power (*Minjung Theology*, p. 58).

In Korea, women constitute a large part of the minjung. It can be said that women are not just one category of minjung, but are also the "minjung of the minjung" in all the other categories. They share a double oppression, first as women, and then as persons who are economically, socially, and politically oppressed. They embody in their suffering the *han* of the Korean people, expressed in sorrow and in the struggle to bring life out of death. As Professor

Park Soon-kyung has put it, women share in all three parts of the "Three Min Struggle": for *minjung* (oppressed people), *minju* (democracy) and *minjok* (nation). The testing ground for the minjung as subjects of their own liberation and theology will be the lives of women seeking to share that vision as full partners.[14]

Authority of Experience

A second theme arising from minjung theology that has many echoes in the stories of women in the USA and Korea is that of the authority of experience. Just as minjung theologians have resisted defining or translating the word "minjung," they have also resisted use of categories of Western theology. Such abstract categories lead them away from the living reality of the minjung. Thus Suh Nam-dong writes about minjung theology as a theology of storytelling: "Originally God's revelation took place among the people of Canaan and Galilee…. It is their stories. It is by no means theology, but their life stories, and, for that matter, it is a counter-theology. It is a counter-theology because the minjung's stories were aimed at criticizing and correcting the ideologies of domination, the ruling system and culture."[15]

By sticking to the stories of the people as an expression of theological insight, the theologians can root their work in the experience of the minjung. This rootage may run the risk of romanticizing minjung, but the danger is avoided by the nature of the stories themselves. For the stories expressed in such forms as *Talch'um* (Masked Dance) and *pansori* (Korean opera) express the self-transcendence of the people as they distance themselves from their religious leaders, rulers and themselves. They reflect a folk culture well aware of the wickedness and greed of humanity. Writing of the mask dance, Hyun Yong-hak says: "They find themselves standing over and beyond the entire work which includes not only the rulers and leaders but also themselves and their own religion" (*Minjung Theology*, p. 50). The social biography of the minjung includes an experience critically reflected upon by those of the minjung who use their art forms and their political actions to resist the oppression of the minjung.

According to Suh Nam-dong, the three most important references for minjung theology's inductive methodology are the events of the exodus and of the crucifixion-resurrection; the history of the church; and the tradition of the minjung movement (*Minjung The-*

ology, pp. 156-157). Here he emphasizes that, unlike the category of "revelation," the category of "reference" makes clear that these are "paradigms" or "archetypes" from historical theology. They can be studied in terms of socioeconomic history and sociology of literature in order to be "...rediscovered and reinterpreted in the context of the human struggle for historical and political liberation today" (*Minjung Theology*, p. 58).

The theological method used in working with these references is summarized by Moon Dong-hwan as including: 1) experience of the minjung analyzed in terms of sociocultural and socioeconomic history; 2) praxis or action/reflection by standing with the minjung and sharing in their struggles; 3) comparing the experience of the minjung with those in other parts of the world and in other previous histories, especially that of the Bible; and 4) storytelling as a means of communication of truth that is not abstract and is immediately understandable to the vast majority of the minjung who have little academic education.[16] As James Cone points out in the preface to *Minjung Theology*, this is not unlike inductive methods used in other liberation/feminist theologies (xvi). Its unique character stems from the use of an inductive method beginning with commitment to act on behalf of the oppressed; using historical-critical critique in a particular context; and developing a community of *koinonia* in which the struggles and stories are celebrated and reflected.

Such an inductive method develops theology or counter-theology out of the experience of the oppressed group. It makes it possible to bring together the dualism between thought and action, as well as those between political and cultural theology. But it still faces the problem of being considered a "non-theology" by the standards of white, male, Western theology because of its appeal to the authority of the experience of the minjung. Classical theology, of course, recognizes that experience is included with biblical and church tradition, and rational analysis in the development of theologies. Yet the abstract paradigm considers experience to be a lesser (practical!) norm, employed only after the theological ideas have been worked out. As Edward Farley has pointed out, classical Christian theology is built on a house of authority that does not allow its system to be verified through experience. Rather it begins with the given norms of revelation and refers all questions about these norms to other rooms in the same closed house.[17]

It seems to me that the reference of counter-theology to the experience of the people's movement in Korea as the source of understanding the "Mission of God in Korea today" demonstrates how the old "house of authority" collapses when it is understood from a sociocritical and sociocultural perspective. I also find the ways in which theological connections are worked out through an appeal to the authority of the oppressed and to their future very helpful for all of us engaged in liberation/feminist theologies. The emphasis on connecting experiences of the oppressed with formal theology through a commitment to praxis is crucial, as is the connecting link made through "messianic politics" (as we shall see in our discussion of the third theme). The use of stories as bearers of this counter-theology provides a rich base for mutual dialogue.

Feminist theologies share with minjung theologies both their appeal to the authority of experience, and their refusal to let the classical norms of theology determine what qualifies as "theology." In this sense feminist theologies are also "counter-theologies," drawing their authority from the experience of women—a group who find themselves discounted as a source of knowledge and understanding, much as the minjung have been discounted as a source of culture and language by rulers and religious leaders in Korea. Their counter-method is to begin with the "hermeneutic of suspicion" which specifies that every theology is biased by its context and by the experience of those shaping the reflection. So they begin with suspicion about what has shaped other theologies (and especially about their patriarchical bias), as well as a commitment to be biased on behalf of full human dignity for women.

Secondly, feminist theologies ask how women's experience functions in shaping theology. Resisting the (so-called) unbiased scientific paradigm of the old "house of authority," they listen to women's stories and analyze the structures that perpetuate violence and alienation in their lives. In order to listen to this counter-constituency, they join forces with other groups to re-discover women's culture and to re-create it through the arts. At the same time they participate in the wider women's movement working for social change. Most importantly for the development of the authority of experience, feminist theologians also take the further step implied in the work of minjung theologians. They value all women and all women's experience and they base the authority of experience, not just on women's experience in general, but on the reflected experience of those who are struggling for equality and mutuality in the present and past. Feminist theology, then, is a theology that appeals to the authority of the experience of struggle against patriarchy and oppression. Through critical reflection, these stories from every nation and denomination provide a *prism* through which God's action in mending creation is to be understood.

An example of such critically reflected stories from the past can be seen in the work of Zora Neale Hurston. A black woman "novelist and folklorist," she died in poverty in 1960 and lay in an unmarked Florida grave until the contemporary black womanist writer, Alice Walker, marked the grave with the epitaph, "Genius of the South."[18] Hurston loved her people and spent her life collecting their stories and tales and weaving them into a lasting legacy of novels and stories. For instance, her essay on High John De Conquer, written in the early 1930s, portrays a black folk savior/hero similar to that of Chang Il-dam in Kim Chi Ha's ballad (*Minjung Theology*, pp. 166-168). High John came to be with the slave folks working on plantations and remained unknown to the white slave masters:

> First off, he was a whisper, a will to hope, a wish to find something worthy of laughter and song. Then the whisper put on flesh. His footsteps sounded across the world in a low but musical rhythm as if the world he walked on was a singing drum. ... John knew that it is written where it cannot be erased, that nothing shall live on human flesh and prosper.[19]

Like the past and present stories, told and retold in Korea, of women factory workers, rural laborers, slum dwellers, victims of tourist prostitution and victims of battering, the stories told in the USA by those who have joined in solidarity with suffering women become a form of exorcism. In Korea this action is familiar in the role of the *mudang* or female shaman who drives out evil spirits and restores harmony in the family and community.[20] In affirming the function of *mudang*, however, women theologians are aware that the exorcism must also cast out the social and political evil along with the more traditional subjective evil. More must be done for the women who come to early morning prayer meetings to pray and weep, having borne the force of their husband's frustration the night before, than simply to exorcise the pent up feelings of *han*. Their exorcism includes the education and legal changes brought about through such work as that of Dr. Lee Tai-young's Legal Aid Center for Family Relations. More must be done with the women factory workers who no longer can get jobs because of their union activities.[21] The work of support and care for one another among widows and wives of those who have been slain or imprisoned becomes an exorcism that leads to sharing not only in prayer but in actions for human rights. These stories and actions form the base of experience for women's theology as an exorcism of patriarchy and all systems of oppression.[22]

Messianic Politics
A third theme from minjung theologians that provides a rich source of dialogue with feminist theologians is that of messianic politics. As in other liberation theologies, eschatology provides the dimension of liberation in the midst of struggle. The articulation of "hope against hope" in situations of "no hope" provides the transcendent dimension of life in the midst of death (Romans 4:18). This dimension is deeply rooted in biblical eschatology, but it also emerges as a ferment of freedom in every part of the globe as people catch the vision of justice, *koinonia* and shalom. In this perspective both minjung and feminist theologians lift up the prophetic-messianic message of the Bible as it is re-incarnated in the lives of women and men today. As Rosemary Ruether has said, "The primary vision of salvation in the Bible is that of an alternative future, a new society of peace and justice that will arise when the present systems of injustice have been overthrown."[23]

In his chapter on "Messiah and Minjung: Discerning Messianic Politics over against Political Messianism," Kim Yong-bock documents the emergence of Korean minjung messianism out of the messianic (*Maitreya*) Buddhism, Donghak egalitarian and ethical religion, and Christianity. This culminated in the "...most dramatic manifestation of minjung messianism in Korea..." during the March First Independence movement of 1919 (*Minjung Theology*, pp. 187-189). Kim sees this independence movement as the "paradigmatic or root experience" of the Korean people. "It supplies the motivation, scope, and direction for the minjung to create their own new future" (*Minjung Theology*, p. 189). He contrasts these movements with the false political messianism of traditional Buddhism, Confucian orthodox political ideology, Japanese ultranationalism, North Korean communism and emerging modern technocracy.

From this documentation it becomes clear that messianic politics is a political process in which the minjung join the messiah in realizing his messianic role. In contrast, political (ruling class) messianism attempts to use and sacrifice the minjung to its own false messianic claims. Kim uses the story of Jesus as the suffering messiah as a paradigm for understanding the collective messianic role of the minjung. This in turn can be interpreted through the messianic traditions of the minjung as we see in Kim Chi Ha's theology of *han* and messianic story of Chang Il-dam (*Minjung Theology*, pp. 178-189).

The concept of messianic politics is of key importance in minjung theology. In spite of the dangers, already mentioned, of collapsing the biblical story of God's liberation totally into the story of the minjung, the use of an eschatological frame of reference provides future transcendence that is always in tension with the present historical reality. This not only links political analysis and sociocultural analysis with the dimension of faith, but also provides a basis for empowerment in the midst of a situation of unresolved resentment against injustices suffered and helplessness against overwhelming odds—a situation of *han*.[24] In "Toward a Theology of *Han*," Suh Nam-dong comments, "*Han* is an underlying feeling of Korean people. On the one hand, it is a dominant feeling of defeat, resignation and nothingness. On the other, it is a feeling with a tenacity of will for life which comes to weaker beings. The first aspect can sometimes be sublimated to great artistic expressions and the second aspect could erupt as the energy for revolution of rebellion."

Minjung theology is a messianic theology built out of the experience of repeated failure and loss among the minjung. With Jesus the theology is downwardly mobile, identifying with the bottom of society and claiming that bottom as what Kim Chi Ha has called "sacred place." It is in the sacred place of imprisonment that he and others have found the power of the weak, the power of a people who never give up. In order to transform that *han* into power for new life Kim Chi Ha has articulated a process of *metanoia* which he calls *dan*. As he discovered in his prison cell, *han* represents a continuing circle of despair, unless the vicious circle of greed which fuels political messianism is cut. He prayed for the power to *dan*, to cut himself off from greed, emulation of the master, and the need for revenge, in order to become identified with minjung messianic deliverance. Such is the commitment of minjung theology: "If one does not hear the sighs of the *han* of the minjung, one cannot hear the voice of Christ knocking on our doors" (*Minjung Theology*, p. 68).

Although feminist theologians in the USA do not usually use the term "messianic politics," their work is very much related to the theme of eschatology. It includes extensive critique of other-worldly eschatology that both overlooks the concrete sufferings of women in patriarchal structures in the present and invites women to wait with patience for the day they will leave their "inferior" bodies and become acceptable to God.[25] Feminist theology appeals to the authority of a future reality of mended creation in which no person is called to dominate as a representative of God. Consequently, this leads to certain reservations about interpreting Genesis 1:28-30 to mean that minjung are partners in subduing the earth.[26] Although such imagery of human subjectivity over history is important for preserving the human dignity of any oppressed group, from a feminist perspective there is danger in this imagery when oppressed males exercise a partnership with God that allows them to subdue and dominate women. Subjectivity at the expense of objects at the bottom is another model of political messianism that is present in most societies.

In the process of advocacy for women, the authority of the future is a key aspect of feminist theologies. Women can appeal to the authority of their experience, but, like the minjung, this experience is primarily of the old creation and of the structures of patriarchy in church and society. We do not yet know what real live children of God will look like! (Rom. 8:19). Therefore, we take the *via negativa* and describe the contradictions of our past and present social, political, economic, and ecclesial experiences. At the same time, we live out of a vision of God's intention for a mended creation and it is this hope that helps us "keep on keeping on." In an important sense Christian feminists *only have this future*, for the patriarchal structures of Scripture, tradition, church and theology are such that the process of reconstruction of woman's place in man's world requires a utopian faith that understands God's future as an impulse for change in the present. As Beverly Harrison has pointed out, the work of feminist theology is not only to identify critically and analyze the past and present order of things, but also to engage in "utopic envisagement."[27]

Most feminist theologians would not say that authority of the future is a key element in their feminist theory. Yet out of the articulation of women's struggles comes a longing for freedom that points to an anticipation of a society that has moved beyond oppression. In my own theory this world beyond oppression is imaged as a mended creation in which human beings, nature and all creation are set free from their groaning. The vision of this partnership of God and all creation is nurtured and anticipated in the *koinonia* women and men form as a community of equals. Elisabeth Schüssler Fiorenza traces this future community, not only in the present, but also in the past community of *women-church*, "...the movement of self-identified women and women-identified men in biblical religion" that she discerns through historical reconstruction of New Testament texts.[28] For her, the discipleship of equals is the eschatological community gathered in response to the power of the resurrection. This community is to live out the teachings of Jesus as anticipations of the Coming One.

Although feminist theologians raise many questions about the "prototype" of a male messiah, and seek to provide ways that the Coming One transcends male/female categories, they do not speak of women collectively in messianic terms. But they do appeal to the authority of their own experience in disclosing the *power of the weak*.[29] They also seek to draw their strength from the bottom of society, especially as imaged in the lives of women crippled by racism and classism. For example, Katie Cannon has pointed out that it is women like Fannie Lou Hamer who image for us what redemption means as it is lived among us.[30] In 1963 this Mississippi sharecropper responded to the call for voter registration and risked her life to register. She was arrested and beaten so viciously that she was permanently debilitated, but she never gave up her struggle for freedom. Fannie Lou Hamer had been to the "bottom" and no one could touch her any more. She only knew the authority of the future's freedom and the journey with others toward that freedom.

Just as the experience of suffering is different in each context the experience of the meaning of an end to that suffering is also interpreted differently. For instance, the element of *dan* as self-denial might find a different emphasis in feminist theology. The experience of many women is that they are given the involuntary role of "self-denial" and "obedience" in society. Therefore, to cut the structures of oppression includes self-assertion, and refusal to live as less than the full human beings God intends women to be. In short, it means cutting across the structures of patriarchy both as they are internalized and as they are lived out in political and economic realities.

Among Korean women theologians the feminist and minjung concerns appear to be coalescing around the themes of powerlessness and *han*. If the existence of women in a Confucian society was *"han"* itself, the only hope for them has been in some form of messianic belief (*Minjung Theology*, p. 58). Yet the transformation of that hope from other-worldly Shamanism calls for a theology of *han* which draws its strength from the transformation of the powerless and *han*-ridden women at the bottom. In their advocacy of these women (such as the factory workers and the prostitutes) the women of the Korean Association of Women Theologians have discovered that it is the "powerless women who are the powerful liberators."[31] The ones who teach us to work for a future when hope is still unseen are the "minjung of the minjung." As Professor Park Soon-kyung said in summarizing the Second Consultation for the Establishment of Feminist Theology in Asia: "Feminist theology cannot be just theory.... We must look at it from the standpoint of laborers and farmers, and then what derives will be a different thing, even though it may look similar."[32]

From time to time in Korea and in other places I have heard it said that Korean women can be minjung theologians only when they learn their theology (*i.e.*, graduate with a Ph.D.). Yet from the point of view of minjung theology itself, women are among the minjung and thus are able to do theology by reflecting on their experience of oppression with or without professional theological education. Even if additional women became professional theologians, the situation of employment for a minjung woman theologian is probably slightly more bleak than for a man.

At other times I have heard that women can be considered minjung theologians when they have been through the experience of going to jail, thereby expressing their commitment to the cause of human rights. Yet women's experience of suffering does not begin with jail. They are born into a society where women are traditionally unwanted, unnamed and subservient in all things to the father, husband, and son.

From my perspective as a white, U.S. feminist, the dialogue must continue among all those who wish to make a commitment to stand in solidarity with the oppressed. And I give thanks to my Third

World brothers and sisters who are making that dialogue a possibility. I look forward to its continuation, not only among all forms of liberation/feminist theologies around the world, but also between the women and men of Korea who seek a way together as minjung.

Notes

1. Proverb quoted by Chung Hyun-kyung at the Consultation of Asian Women Theologians, "Doing Theology from an Asian Women's Perspective," February 22-23, 1985, Mercy Center, Madison, Connecticut. As Chung Hyun-kyung pointed out at the meeting, their purpose was to *break a lot of plates*! After sharing the theological papers, Bible study, cultural celebrations, and gatherings for worship, I could only believe that this was a true description of the transformation that was beginning to come about. And I look forward to a time in the very near future when Korean women themselves will publish, not one chapter about women's perspectives on minjung theologies, but entire books! Without this contribution in partnership with other minjung theologians, the theology itself will contain a basic contradiction, for its subject will be the minjung but the "minjung of the minjung" will not be articulating and interpreting their own stories.

2. *Third Eye Theology* (Maryknoll, N.Y.: Orbis Books, 1979), p. 3.

3. *Minjung Theology: People as the Subjects of History* (Maryknoll, London, Singapore: Orbis, Zed, CCA, 1983), pp. 16-17. Because of the frequency with which I refer to this volume, all further references to *Minjung Theology* will be included in the text.

4. Pointed out by Chung Hyun-kyung at a conference on "Global Women Theologians in Dialogue," Stony Point, N.Y., January 15-16, 1986.

5. "The Role of Asian Women Theologians Studying/Working in the USA," The Claremont School of Theology, November 22-23, 1985.

6. Park Sun-ai, "Introduction to the Report on the Asian Women's Consultation" (EATWOT *Pro Mundi Vita*) (February 1986). See "Women in Third World Theology," *Voices from the Third World* (EATWOT, Vol. VIII:3) (September 1985), Asian Theology Centre, 281 Deans Road, Colombo 10, Sri Lanka.

7. "Second Consultation for the Establishment of Feminist Theology in Asia: Our Confession," and "General Comments," by Rev. Chung Sook-ja. *In God's Image* (December 1984), pp. 19-23. See also *In God's Image* (April 1985), pp. 30-31.

8. *In God's Image*, p. 5.

9. Letty M. Russell, "Reflections from a First World Perspective," *Doing Theology in a Divided World*, ed. by Virginia Fabella and Sergio Torres (Maryknoll, N.Y.: Orbis, 1985).

10. *Fire beneath the Frost*, by Peggy Billings with Moon Tong Hwan, Han Wan Sang, Son Myong Gul, Pharis Harvey (New York: Friendship Press, 1984), p. 9. See also Suh Kwang-sun David, "Theology of Storytelling: A Theology by Minjung," *Ministerial Formation*, Programme on Theological Education, WCC, Vol. 31 (September 1985), pp. 10-22.

11. *All the Women Are White, All the Blacks Are Men, But Some of Us Are Brave: Black Women's Studies*, ed. by Gloria T. Hull, Patricia Bell Scott, and Barbara Smith (Old Westbury, N.Y.: The Feminist Press, 1982), p. 49.

12. *Bread Not Stone* (Boston: Beacon Press, 1984) p. xiv.

13. "Defining the Problem: The Bible and Feminist Hermeneutics," *SEMEIA* 28: The Bible and Feminist Hermeneutics, Society of Biblical Literature (1983), p. 120.

14. Quoted from an informal conversation at the Commission on Faith and Order, WCC, Stavanger, Norway, August 12-26, 1986.

15. *In Search of Minjung Theology* (Seoul: Hankilsa, 1984), pp. 305-306. Translated and quoted by Suh Kwang-sun David in "Theology of Storytelling: A Theology by Minjung," p. 20.

16. "Korean Minjung Theology: An Introduction," *Korean-American Relations at Crossroads*, ed. by Wonmo Dong (Princeton, N.J.: The Association of Korean Christian Scholars in North America, Inc., 1982), pp. 14-16.

17. *Ecclesial Reflection: An Anatomy of Theological Method* (Philadelphia: Fortress Press, 1982), pp. 165-68.

18. Alice Walker, *In Search of Our Mother's Gardens: Womanist Prose* (San Diego: Harcourt Brace Jovanovich, 1983), p. 107.

19. Zora Neale Hurston, *The Sanctified Church* (Berkeley: Turtle Island, 1983), pp. 69, 71.

20. Moon, *Fire beneath the Frost*, p. 25. See also "Lowborn Women of Influence," *Women of Korea: A History of Ancient Times to 1945*, ed. by Kim Yung-chung (Seoul: Ewha Womans University Press, 1982), pp. 129-144. See Lee Oo-chung, *Women's History, 100 Years* (Seoul: Christian Missions Study Center, 1985 [in Korean]).

21. Cho Wah-soon, *Christ among the Minjung: A Woman's Witness*, unpublished. See also "Cho Wha-soon: A Modern Apostle," *Fire beneath the Frost*, pp. 58-65. Also Pak Young-mi, "The Role of Labor Unions in the Female Labor Movement in South Korea," *Korea Scope*, Vol. III:3 (December 1983), pp. 3-12.

22. The idea of women's theology as a form of exorcism was discussed at the Stony Point conference on "Global Women Theologians in Dialogue."

23. "A Religion for Women: Sources and Strategies," *Christianity and Crisis*, Vol. 39:19 (December 10, 1979), p. 309.

24. *Fire beneath the Frost*, p. 4.

25. Rosemary Radford Ruether, "Eschatology and Feminism," *Sexism and God-Talk: Toward a Feminist Theology* (Boston: Beacon Press, 1983), pp. 235-238.

26. Phyllis Trible, *God and the Rhetoric of Sexuality* (Philadelphia: Fortress Press, 1978), pp. 12-23.

27. Beverly Wildung Harrison, *Our Right to Choose: Toward a New Ethics of Abortion* (Boston: Beacon Press, 1983), p. 285.

28. *Bread Not Stone*, pp. xiv-xvii. See also Elisabeth Schüssler Fiorenza, *In Memory of Her: A Feminist Theological Reconstruction of Christian Origins* (New York: Crossroad, 1983), pp. 285-342.

29. Elizabeth Janeway, *Powers of the Weak* (New York: Morrow Quill, 1981).

30. Katie Cannon, "Rage and Redemption: Experiences of the Black Church," An oral presentation for the Women's Theological Center (Boston, MA: April 26, 1985). See also *When and Where I Enter*, pp. 289-290.

31. Henna Yeogumhyun Han, "The Powerless Women as the Powerful Liberators," Unpublished paper for Feminist Hermeneutics (Yale Divinity School, Fall, 1985).

32. *In God's Image*, p. 34.

An Old Woman
(Taken from the story of Changma in Yun Hyong-kil's *Rainy Season*)

There was an old woman who lived on a farm and had two sons. The older son married and went to live with his mother-in-law's family in Seoul. During the Korean war he, along with his wife and mother-in-law, moved back to the farm and stayed in the outer part of his mother's house. His mother, the old woman, and his mother-in-law did not get along. One of the reasons they did not get along had to do with their sons. During the war one of the mother-in-law's sons, a university graduate, was killed by communist guerrillas. During this same war, the old woman's youngest son, an uneducated farmer, joined the communist guerrillas. Whenever the old woman worried about her son living the dangerous life of a guerrilla in the mountains, the mother-in-law was angered and was filled with hatred.

One day the old woman decided to go to a fortuneteller to find out when her younger son would return home. The fortuneteller told her the date of her son's return. To welcome his homecoming, she asked her older son and his mother-in-law to prepare food. When the day came, instead of her son, a huge snake appeared in the yard. Upon seeing the snake, the old woman fainted. The snake climbed a persimmon tree and looked down at the old woman. Although everyone else was frightened, the mother-in-law alone was calm. She brought food to the table and placed it before the snake and said: "You have come all the way to see your mother. Do not worry. Your old brother will take care of her. Eat and enjoy this food prepared for you and go away." Hearing this the snake came down from the tree and slithered off into the bamboo forest behind the house. When the old woman recovered consciousness, she asked, "Is he gone?" The mother-in-law said "Yes." Since then they became good friends. A few days later the old woman died.

Black Theology
and Minjung Theology:
Exploring Common Themes
by J. Deotis Roberts

This discussion is an exercise in cross-cultural theological conversation. In this paper I explore some common themes in two theological traditions which may be designated generally as "liberation theologies." But this language may be deceptive. I do not consider Latin American liberation theology as emblematic of this truly global movement. It appears to me that black theology and minjung theology have more in common than some other options in liberation theology, such as those emanating from Latin America.

It may be necessary to indicate that black theology itself is not monolithic. Black theology is based upon black religious experience, black culture, and the black church tradition. It is a unity-in-diversity. Black theologians differ in their perceptions of a common tradition, and their intellectual and spiritual journeys are richly varied. In a broad sense, Howard Thurman and Martin Luther King, Jr., were black theologians whose work grew out of the black experience, experience which has become so crucial to contemporary black theology. While much of contemporary black theological thought is based upon "a political model," some of the earlier work focused on *ethical* and *cultural* concerns. It is my view that black theology should be broadly conceived, encompassing a strong emphasis upon history and culture, without toning down the essential, political liberation thrust.

This more comprehensive view, which balances cultural and political interest, has the advantage of a strong affinity to both African and Asian theological developments. The political model, for example, relates directly to the South African situation, where emphasis on eradicating racial apartheid has become a central concern in black theological thought. Yet, as John Mbiti of Kenya reminds us, the political emphasis does not resonate as strongly in most other parts of Africa, which have already achieved independence and are now examining post-colonial issues. I have adopted this more comprehensive view, in an attempt to provide a more serious response to minjung theology.

Reflection on Roots
A logical place to begin is with the similarities in history and culture between black theology and minjung theology.

Since the early 1960s, the rise of black theology has been given serious attention in the USA by several religious and secular scholars. While it is not necessary to chronicle this history here, a brief review may be helpful.

Most Afro-Americans came to North America from West Africa, though some certainly came from other parts of the continent. Enslaved, they lived principally on plantations of the South, where they toiled in the cotton fields and were forced to perform other agricultural chores. The experience of bondage was their stark introduction to the New World. They were uprooted from their history and culture by a brutal system which bound them for generations.

This tortured experience followed them right up to the middle of the nineteenth century, until the time of Emancipation, when they were officially declared free. Unfortunately, the action taken to free blacks through the Civil War and the freedom documents did not uproot racial segregation, or the ugly reality of racism. As a consequence, the black struggle continues. Even in the twilight of the twentieth century, there is no discernable solution to this problem. In fact, there is a serious indication that the gains we, as blacks, have made during the last twenty-five years are being eroded. In a real sense, blacks still live in the shadow of slavery.

Black theology arose out of an upsurge of black consciousness and power in the late 1960s. It was a combined search for cultural roots and the power or means of liberation from racist oppression. It continued the "stride toward freedom" thrust of Martin Luther King, Jr.'s project. The new movement had both continuity and discontinuity with the work of Dr. King. It was the culmination of more than two centuries of struggle.

A similar history has prompted the emergence of minjung theology. Korea has been caught in the viselike grip of the great Asian powers for many centuries. It has been in the crossfire of conflicts between Russia, China and Japan. This has led to much suffering for the Korean people. In the early twentieth century, Korea was a colony of Japan. This was followed by a communist invasion and the partitioning of the country into north and south, the bitter fruit of a tragic war involving the USA as well as other nations. In the period since that tragedy, South Korea has witnessed several oppressive governments. It is, in a real sense, a national security state, with frequent infringements upon human rights. The majority of the Korean people have been victimized by these crucial historical realities. They have had to search for meaning and seek survival under these repressive circumstances.

The history of suffering has run parallel to the Christian missionary movement. First the Roman Catholic church established itself in Korea. This was followed by the Protestant missionary effort which has been present in Korea for about a century. Owing to the Korean experience of so much mass suffering from political oppression, the gospel took on a prophetic as well as a priestly connotation from its introduction to Korea through the Christian missionary movement of the last century.

Afro-Asian worldviews are essentially holistic. Christianity encounters, therefore, in both the Korea and black theological developments, non-Western foundations. Blacks are Afro-Americans. Black theology affirms African roots. Minjung theology is built upon pre-Christian religious, ethical and cultural factors. Apart from traditional African cultural and religious traits, it is not possible to have an in-depth understanding of black theology, the black church, or black family and cultural traditions. Confucianism, Buddhism, Shamanism and other elements are essential to the Korean context. These are related to the development of minjung theology. Finally, there is a holism in the African and Asian worldviews which may account for a real affinity between blacks and Koreans in their way of developing theological thought. For example, in both cases there is a ready acceptance of the exodus paradigm in doing theology.

Response to Oppression: People as Subjects of History

One of the most difficult tasks for a people victimized by a situation of oppression is to find a constructive, nonviolent response. By nonviolence, I am suggesting a form of action rather than silent resignation. It is easier to resort to fatalism or violent revolution than it is to formulate a plan for massive resistance against structural evil though nonviolent means. This is why the work of Martin Luther King, Jr., has such worldwide significance. Even though the method was introduced by Gandhi, it was given its classic expression in the Christian love ethic by King. But before developing this further, it is necessary to unpack the meaning of the theme of this section: "people as subjects of history."

David Shanon, a black biblical scholar and educator, strongly emphasizes the need for Afro-Americans to become "subjects" rather than "objects" of history. This observation grew out of his recent experience as president of Virginia Union University. What he meant was that Afro-Americans need a new mind-set. The Reagan administration in the United States has withdrawn much support from persons who have been victimized and handicapped by a long history of oppression, whether black, hispanic, Native American, female, or elderly. This means that they will be defeated by circumstances unless they take their destinies into their own hands. While I am aware that this expectation is difficult when one has suffered a depletion of material and psychological resources, it does seem to be an essential posture for the underclasses in U.S. society. Afro-Americans are in a position where not only social services and educational opportunities are being curtailed, but "affirmative action" is being phased out as well. Even programs designed to train people to work have suffered a setback as a result of new priorities, especially militarism.

Some blacks have resigned themselves to what they consider the fate of alienation and suffering. Rampant unemployment has led to alcohol and drug abuse and all types of personal and familial tragedies. Others have turned to the solace of religion. Emotional and other-worldly aspects of religion have provided compensation for those who are denied the fulfillment of life here and now. But, on the other hand, there has emerged also from the resources of religion advocates of social justice who have given black people the courage to claim their dignity and struggle for freedom in spite of their hopelessness. Religious faith can provide "resources of grace" that enable people who are by circumstances "objects" of history the means to become "subjects" of history. This is in essence what the "exodus" theme in black religious history is all about.

It seems to me that this concern to become subjects rather than objects of history brings black and minjung theologies together at a vital point. This perspective has been looked at over a long period of time. It has resurfaced in many parts of the world. It was especially prevalent in countries moving from colonialism into independence, development and liberation. The writings of Franz Fanon are noteworthy in this regard. Paulo Freire's writings on consciousness-raising have been celebrated, not only in Latin America, but worldwide. A people who internalize their desire to be free are not easily enslaved. A veteran, reflecting upon his experience, observed that from the first engagement with the Viet Cong, he knew that they would likely win the war, owing to their determination. They were programed psychologically and ideologically not to be defeated. When a people change from being objects of history to being subjects of their history, they become a force to reckon with. They are motivated from within and are prepared to confront any odds in the quest for liberation.

The Korean people compare their experience with that of the Israelites of the Bible. So much of their history seems to parallel that of the Hebrews. As mentioned earlier, Korea has been the battleground of the great nations of the Far East. Their geopolitical reality has been shaped by the interests of Asian imperial states and, more recently, by those of the USA. The theme of the exodus and the message of the prophets of social justice help to define their reality. They see the divine hand reaching into their history as it did in the early history of the Hebrew people.

In this regard there is a similarity between the experience of Afro-Americans and Koreans in the manner in which they have understood and appropriated the message of the Bible. In both cases the leadership style of Moses and theme of the exodus have been freighted with great meaning of freedom from oppression. The slave songs, especially the spirituals, have taken up this message in a powerful way. Thus it seems to me that the religious and theological responses to oppression have been similar in the Korean and Afro-American situations.

The Meaning of the Cross
Because of the common experience of suffering, black theology and minjung theology focus strongly upon the meaning of suffering. Theodicy is a controlling category. The problem of structural evil and the consequence of mass suffering is inescapable. The only viable option is in the response to this reality. It can be met with resignation as well as skepticism or it can be translated into a source of strength.

It seems to me that recent black theologians as well as minjung theologians, upon contextualizing the experience of suffering, have elected to transform it. They not only accept it as a given, but they seek to transmute it into a source of moral and spiritual resistance to evil. They do not attempt this out of defiance as some existentialists (such as Albert Camus) have done. Neither do they accept the "humaneo-centric" approach of William Jones in *Is God a White Racist?* (Garden City, N.Y.: Doubleday, 1973). They do, though, adopt a christocentric model, for the most part. In both cases the Jesus of history is also the Christ of faith.

In developing an approach to evil and suffering, they are moved to re-examine their christology. Minjung theologians have examined the message of Jesus to the poor. They have sought a deep understanding of the Jesus of history and the secular meaning of the Gospel. (Bonhoeffer's writings have been very helpful as a backdrop to much reflection on the life of Jesus and the meaning of his cross.)

Concurrently, black theologians have sought after the Jesus of the "disinherited." The adoption of the symbol of the "Black Messiah" has surfaced as a way of dealing with the self-identity crisis and the situation of racism and poverty. In other words, there has been an examination of traditional christological models, but with a view to how these may speak more forcefully to the reality of black suffering based on the experience of continuous oppression. Again this has led to a serious engagement with the cross of Christ.

In black and minjung theological programs, there is a reluctance to dwell upon the regal or kingly role of Jesus. The stress upon the resurrection does not overshadow the weight given to the cross of Christ. The lordship of Jesus so easily underwrites a situation of domination of the weak by the powerful. Emphasis upon the resurrection easily points to other-worldliness and triumphalism to the disadvantage of any oppressed group. I see in black and minjung theologies an emphasis upon Jesus' cross and this leads to a balanced view of the resurrection, for there is no resurrection without a cross. The regal role of Jesus is brought into a dynamic relation with his priestly and prophetic ministry. I do not see the absence of a well-rounded christological model; it is more a matter of emphasis and balance.

A christological model which is either other-worldly or only regal is generally acceptable to a repressive order. It does not challenge the established order in violation of human rights for the mass of humanity suffering from oppressions such as poverty or racism. It does not speak redemptively to the underclass. The tendency, therefore, is for the privileged class to enthrone a regal Christ as the sanctifier of the status quo. Those who see Christ as the liberator are likely to be subject to denunciation and persecution by those in power. This is why black as well as minjung theologians have chosen a different dimension of christology in which the cross is central. But the cross is not a symbol of escape; it is rather a symbol of engagement with evil and suffering. Christ's victorious resurrection is seen in relation to the cross as its sequel and ultimate vindication.

Conclusion

This brief excursion into comparative theology has been a challenge. It is highly suggestive of the rich possibilities toward human understanding which could result from vigorous activity on this theological frontier. In a comparison of black and minjung theologies, we note important differences. But our concern has been to highlight the similarities.

We have drawn upon the affinity of worldviews among Afro-Americans and Asians. There is also a cluster of similar factors in both backgrounds which result in a holistic ethico-religious outlook. When we translate this into biblical terms, it leads to a view which blends social justice concerns with the healing dimensions of the gospel. In both instances the exodus theme points to the message of the prophets of the Hebrew Scriptures who denounced oppression and advocated justice as well as mercy. Again, both black and minjung theologies seek to find the historical Jesus and the secular meaning of the gospel for human liberation. This in no way dilutes the meaning and power associated with the cross-resurrection event. The Christ of faith is Lord, but he is also Liberator. In these and other ways black and minjung theologies may open new doors to cross-cultural understanding and the ecumenical dialogue and mission of the church of Jesus Christ.

The Story of Simchung
(From a popular folk tale)

Once upon a time there was a blind man, known by the name of Sim Bong-sa, who lived with his daughter Simchung. When Simchung was a baby, her mother died. It came to pass that the blind father had to beg for milk and food to raise his daughter.

When Simchung became a teenager, she decided to work for other people as a maid, thereby supporting her blind father. One day she had to work late and did not come home on time. The blind father worried and went out to search for his daughter. Because he was unfamiliar with the roads he was on, he fell into a ditch. A monk who passed by rescued him. Knowing he was blind, the monk promised to restore his sight if he would offer three hundred bags of rice to the Buddhist temple. Upon hearing this story, Simchung prayed and prayed for the three hundred bags of rice that would open her father's eyes.

One day she heard that the sailors of a merchant ship from Nanking were looking for a sixteen-year-old girl to be used as a sacrifice to the spirit of water. This sacrifice would quiet the ocean. Simchung exchanged herself for three hundred bags of rice, which were sent to the Buddhist temple. The poor blind man was filled with joy when he was informed that the three hundred bags of rice were sent to the temple. He did not learn the real story until the full moon appeared and the sailors came to take Simchung away. The blind father did not want to let her go and held on to her tightly. But it was no use. Simchung was already sold for the three hundred bags of rice.

When the ship was in the middle of the ocean, a storm suddenly arose. The sailors knew that the sea-ghosts were coming after them. They then threw Simchung into the water. A large fish came and took her into the bottom of the sea, where the dragon-king dwelt. Seeing the beauty of this girl, the dragon-king adopted her as his own daughter.

In spite of the splendid life in the dragon palace, Simchung was unhappy. She thought of her blind father on earth. The dragon-king seeing her sadness decided to send her back to earth. She was placed in a lotus flower and floated on the surface of the sea. At that time a prince of the kingdom was sailing along and saw a beautiful girl peeping out from the lotus flower. The prince instantly fell in love with her and decided to marry her.

A great wedding feast was planned. For many days and nights people came to the festivities. After the wedding a great feast was held for all the blind men in the country. Hundreds and thousands of blind men came to the feast and finally the last day Sim Bong-sa appeared. With unspeakable joy Simchung ran and embraced him and cried, "Father! Father!" Hearing the voice of his daughter, the blind man also cried with joy. At that very moment of great excitement his eyes were opened and he saw for the first time his beautiful daughter.

The Religion of Ordinary People: Toward a North American Minjung Theology

by Harvey Cox

The only time I ever met Dorothy Day, foundress of the Catholic Worker Movement, she told me she'd recently been quite impressed by a song from a Broadway musical. The song was called, "What Do the Simple Folk Do?" Over the past twenty-five years, I have come to believe that the religion of ordinary people, the "simple folk," though often misused for domination, holds enormous potential for liberation. This means a principal theological task becomes sorting out the liberative from the manipulative elements in a religious heritage.

One thing such a task suggests for Christian theologians is that the whole Christian tradition itself has to be constantly reviewed and understood from a critical perspective, which is in part informed by the Bible. (That's what the Reformation was about.) As for the relationship of Christianity to other world religions, my own conviction is that one can better enter into this discussion as a serious but *critical* participant in one's own tradition than as one trying to stand above or combine them all.

I say that, not just out of theological reflection, but out of some real experience in the inter-faith dialogue. I have lived in a Krishna temple in India and I have lectured to Buddhists in Japan. My experience is that the mystery of faith and the mystery of God come to us in a very particular form. I am distrustful of a kind of academic distancing from everything so that one can allegedly "see it all." I don't think that's the way people of faith know and appreciate each other's traditions. I can converse with a conservative Baptist like Jerry Falwell or a Tibetan Buddhist like Chogyam Trumgpa because of a certain shared intuition that we are really critical *participants* in these different traditions. That awakens a kind of recognition.

But what do we mean by critical participant? The minjung idea teaches us that we have to be self-critical about what aspects of our own or other traditions we affirm. This requires us to avoid the "religion of the rulers" and to seek out the minjung. When we do this the dialogue will be both *practical* and *conflictual* since that is the way the minjung live.

When one looks at minjung and the various liberation theologies from the angle of Western academic theology, one sees that they raise enormously critical issues for the next decades of Christian theology. The fact is that the demographic center of Christianity is rapidly shifting to the black, brown, yellow, poor southern hemisphere. This means that our millennium-long habit of thinking of Christianity as being somehow centered in Europe, with branch offices around the world, is dying. It will not be that way anymore and, frankly put, many of the churches in the Third World think of this movement away from European thought patterns as a great liberation. They rejoice that they no longer need to think like little Europeans in order to become Christian theologians. So the "De-Europeanizing" of Christianity is one of the things at stake in the emergence of minjung theology. (One of the theologians I met in Brazil called this process *des-nortificacao*, the "de-Northification" of the gospel.) What does the gospel look like when it's been unwrapped from its northern, European shell and allowed to take root and flower in a quite other culture?

Emerging from this shell reminds us how once a basically Hebrew perspective on reality, having to do with love and faith and community, became translated into the Hellenistic perspective. This in turn became for Western Christians the exclusive perspective for understanding their faith. Christianity was thus understood primarily in terms of doctrinal formulations; this has become so commonplace it seems completely natural to us. "What is it to be a Christian? It's to believe ABCD." If you're in one branch, you believe twenty-six things and in another one it's perhaps only three things. But this idea that the central spine of Christianity entails giving consent to a body of doctrines seems so utterly unquestionable to us that we forget it is really a product of the Hellenistic milieu of the first formative centuries of Western Christianity.

Theology, however, as minjung theologians and other Third World theologians remind us, is a form of reflection that is secondary to the primary activity of the community of faith: prayer, witness, service, prophecy, martyrdom, and celebration. Theology does not create itself. It is a critical, constructive commentary on something else. In the modern period, however, we have evolved a social location for theologizing which is in some measure insulated from the primary experience on which theology reflects. In the USA and Canada, for example, most theologians are paid by academic institutions, where there is often a certain suspicion or even condescension toward communities of faith.

No doubt it was once liberating for theology to get out from under rigid ecclesial control. But being housed in the mental world of the modern university presents its own, often less visible, restrictions and obstacles. If one is not careful one can end up writing exclusively for other people who are in this so-called theological world, which really means the world of faculties and of professional associations of trained theologians.

One of the critical lessons of liberation theology is the painful discovery on the part of one person after another that the social standing, and not simply the geographical location, of the theologian is enormously important. Modern North Atlantic theology justifiably prides itself on its critical method. But there is a continuing blind spot in this critical stance when it comes to this question of the "social location" of the theologian and the impact of this location on one's work. What problems present themselves? What agenda suggests itself as the one to work on? To whom do you feel responsible or accountable for what you do? All these questions tend to be answered by the social location.

There would not be any liberation theology if liberation theologians were still living in a kind of splendid isolation. One after another, they report that they had to undergo a major change in the way they work and in the way they think, because of their involvement with the people in the grassroots, with the base communities and popular movements.

In short, what is special about liberation theology has to do with a new kind of collaboration between the theologian and the community of faith—a community made up principally of the poor.

While I don't accept the romantic notion that liberation theology arises entirely from the poor and oppressed, and all the liberation theologians did was to write it down, it is a fact that oppressed Christians in Latin America are not just an audience. They are also in some way *participants* in the construction of this theological movement. It is the combination of these two elements—

theologians trained in modern critical theology, and "minjung" piety faced with painful life situations—that creates liberation theology. The coming together of these two elements holds much promise for the future.

Liberation theology is often perceived as being very political, in a confrontational sense. But there is much more to liberation theology than "politics." There is also a form of spirituality emerging from this movement. When Pope John XXIII called the Second Vatican Council, he said it was his hope that the council would "enable the church to become what she really is, namely, a church of the poor." Liberation theology begins with the church's "preferential option for the poor." One can interpret that many ways. For the liberation theologians, it means the poor ought to form a kind of core conscience of the church. The poor should provide the heartbeat for the whole people of God, a kind of mystery in which Christ himself is present in a special way.

Liberation theology is principally a way of looking at the gospel and the Christian tradition from the perspective of the poor, so everything in that tradition—modes of discipline, forms of prayer, sacraments, devotional exercises and so on—can all be seen and reclaimed and purified. Let me take an example and suggest how liberation theology deals with it. The idea that *baptism* is the visible sign by which someone enters into the life of Christ— his ministry, suffering and death—has to be informed theologically by Christ's own identification with those who were the poor and oppressed of his own time. Baptism requires a "theology of recapitulation," the taking upon oneself of the vocation, the ministry, the project of Jesus Christ himself. It is this which makes one a part of the community he called into being.

This is a rather different understanding of baptism than the one that sees it exclusively as a cleansing from original sin. It is also different from those views of baptism which see it as a sign that this person is now a part of a community but that do not elicit any particular responsibility on the part of the person for participating in the ongoing ministry of Christ in the world. This liberationist view of baptism may sound new. But it has old visible sources in Catholic theological history and development. (I would also argue that it is in faithful continuity with the theology of Vatican Council II.)

As a U.S. theologian, I would like to suggest that the idea of the faith of the minjung also has an important bearing on U.S.-Soviet relations. During a recent visit to the Soviet Union, I found that the animating passions of the Russian people come from their attachment to Russian history, their affection for their homeland, and their ambivalent criticism of the regime that has defined so much of their existence. All this has a lot to do with the effort of the Soviet people to recover in some measure the profoundly Christian themes and ideas of the Russian novelistic tradition, represented by Fyodor Dostoyevski and others, which is profoundly Christian, and the humanistic tradition of Russian literature and music.

Many Americans are only recently becoming aware of the vitally persistent life of the Christian churches in Russia. But these Christians have something to say to their counterparts in the West, although I'm at a bit of a loss to know how to put it. The Polish writer Czeslaw Milosz discusses the way so many intellectual currents that began in the West became almost a decimating plague when they reached the East. All these ideas—rationalism, science, progress—were taken up with enormous intensity. Milosz believes Russian writers, especially Dostoyevski, saw the long-term consequences of the Enlightenment, of rationalism, faith in science, and progress. He claims that Dostoyevski, writing from a kind of Russian minjung perspective, foresaw an inevitable collision between these "enlightened" ideas and Christian truth. He wrote about it with such intensity that it seemed to be bordering on pathology—or perhaps, prophecy. One hundred years after Dostoyevski, we live in a period in which it seems quite evident that ideas he warned us about are leading toward something unspeakably destructive.

The palace of science has not been our salvation. Technology has been put to demonic purposes. Hope for progress is something that hardly anybody seriously affirms anymore. And we're left with a kind of emptiness, a spiritual hunger that Dostoyevski himself felt and anticipated, and a sense that his message of Christianity, which is the coming of God into the life of humankind, in a man who suffered and died to infuse humanity with the spirit of God, is what has to be reclaimed.

Would it not be ironic if in the next century a revival of Christianity occurred stemming from the Union of Soviet Socialist Republics? I fantasize about this sometimes. The three countries in the world with the largest Christian populations are the United States, Brazil and the USSR. I am sympathetic with those people in the USSR who are critical of the Soviet system without falling into illusions about the West. They have something important to teach us.

Finally, at the risk of sounding too "denominational," let me say why the idea of minjung faith has helped me to decide, despite everything, to remain a Baptist. It is not just that I believe most of the things Baptists have traditionally stood for, such as the importance of the local worshiping community, the emphasis on the Bible, the centrality of Jesus Christ. It is also because it is a severely nonhierarchical conception of the church. Moreover, being a Baptist gives me an important relationship to the largest body of black Christians in the United States. Dorothy Day once said she became a Catholic in part because it was, in the USA, the religion of the poor. One could say the same about Baptists.

I also resonate in my own theology with the theology of the black churches because of the continuing centrality of Jesus one finds there. Jesus was himself, after all, a part of the minjung, and that may be why the figure of Jesus continues to exert such power over my own understanding of myself and of the world and of the nature of God. The content of that influence can change, and has changed over the years, but the figure remains, the person remains, the influence remains. I've always had problems, sometimes major ones, with the word "savior," because I know that that kind of language came into the New Testament from a worldview that I don't find myself in complete sympathy with now. But I think the word "savior" still carries with it one positive note. It says that in the future of Jesus Christ we are dealing with the disclosure in our own history of something ultimate. In Jesus we are face to face with God, and there isn't god above God.

We surely have minjung faith in the USA, but we do not yet have a real minjung "theology." We lack it in part because of the religious and political isolation within which most of our theologians work. If we can begin to break down that isolation, to learn from the trust in Jesus of the black churches, the Dostoyevskian passion of the Russian believers, and other expressions of minjung faith, then something quite significant could begin to happen.

ASIAN
PERSPECTIVES

민중신학

The Story of Wangnyon
(From the novel *Shingung* [God's Bow] by Chon Seung-se, 1977)

Wangnyon was a famous shaman who lived in a small fishing village on the island Chang-sungpo, located on the southwest coast of the Korean peninsula. Her mother-in-law as well as her daughter-in-law were also shamans. Because she made enough money from her shamanistic practices, Wang-nyon decided to get a nice fishing boat for her husband. Her husband, however, was unable to catch any fish. Because of unsuccessful fishing for three years, Wang-nyon and her husband had to borrow money from a rich usurer known as Pansu. Being wicked and immoral, Pansu took away the boat to cover their debts. Wang-nyon became deeply distressed and was unable to perform any shamanistic rituals. Pansu, however, requested her to perform a shamanistic ritual for good fishing. She refused at first because she did not want to have anything to do with him. Then she suddenly received the spirit and went into a trance. She began to perform a shamanistic ritual. In the midst of this ritual, she placed a bowl on Pansu's head and shot the poisoned arrow from God's bow and killed him instantly. Thus she became a heroine of the oppressed people.

Building a Theological Culture of People

by C.S. Song

This reflection is dedicated to the memory of Professor Suh Nam-dong, director of Institute for Mission Education of the Presbyterian church in the Republic of Korea until his sudden death on July 19, 1984.

A perceptive theologian and an initiator of minjung theology, he was arrested, tortured, and imprisoned for his struggle for human rights. A warm and sincere Christian devoted to the cause of love, justice and freedom, Professor Suh lived his theology within the turbulent life of his own nation and underwent the suffering of Jesus in the suffering of his own people.

His theological legacy will be the ongoing quest of "people" theology in Korea and elsewhere in Asia.

The Christian faith can be a dynamic force in social and political life in Korea. It can break out of self-imposed isolation from the world and make its impact felt on the conscience of the nation. It can ask disturbing questions that compel rulers and ruled alike to face real issues and concerns. It can be inspired to take sides, not the side of the rich and the powerful, but the side of the poor and the humiliated.

Minjung theology has made its indelible mark on the social and political ethos of the people of Korea in the teeth of misunderstanding, calumny and pressures both inside and outside the church. Many of its advocates have gone through the experiences of harassment, torture and imprisonment. They were expelled from teaching in universities and seminaries. Suffering, the mark of minjung, and of course the supreme mark of the cross of Jesus, ceased to be a concept to be theologically analyzed and metaphysically contemplated. It became part of their lived experience. It even became a bill of rights, so to speak, for any one aspiring to do theology in any authentic way. Suffering must not be idolized. But suffering in the body and in the spirit gives a quality lacking in most conventional theology. Minjung theology is a theology of the cross.

But it is not their suffering that minjung theologians talk about in their theological experience. Suffering is the suffering of minjung: men, women and children who live in slums, people who are economically exploited, human beings deprived of their social and political rights. In the words of Suh Nam-dong, "Those who witness to the Gospel are not only prophets but also priests....The priestly function is not to give comfort to the rich and the powerful and bless their oppressive power and exploitation. It is not to hypnotize the oppressed and put their resistance forces to sleep. Truly, it is the job of the priests to take care of the wounds of the minjung and enable them to restore their self-respect and courage, and to respond to their historical aspiration."[1]

An "Unfashionable" Theology

Minjung theologians have to be theologians speaking out of the experience of people who suffer, and speaking to those who inflict suffering on the people. Theirs is not a "new" theology. It is as old as the Hebrew Scriptures. Theirs is not a "fashionable" theology. It is in fact as "unfashionable" as that of Jesus two thousand years ago. Jesus had to stare the cross in the face. They had to count on police interference in their theological efforts.

Minjung theology is then a political theology; it is not theological politics. It does not play politics: it does not say "Peace, Peace!" when there is no peace. It does not give a false diagnosis affirming that all is well when not all is well. That is why it listens to the pulse of the people with great attentiveness. It strains its ears to hear the words spoken in their secret hearts. It tries to read their minds hidden behind their impassive faces. It seeks to understand what it hears with a mind sharpened by the mind of Jesus. It does not stop there, however. It does its best to point up political implications of what it has understood theologically.

Minjung theology thus affirms people as the subject of history. Its task is to give an account of history as "the sociopolitical biography" of the people.[2] It has proceeded to open a Pandora's box of Korean history. And with fascination and dismay it listens to the *han* of the restless souls crying out of the depths of the history buried in the past of the nation. It also sees deep down in the hearts of men, women and children today the suppressed *han* vainly struggling to be vindicated.

In theology, the minjung have emerged from the subconsciousness of history and broken out of imprisonment in the subterranean region hidden from the social and political life of the nation. This is liberation! The minjung are now a social and political power to be reckoned with. This strongly points to inevitable transformations in social structures and political decision-making processes. That "minjung-people are the subjects of history" is not just theological jargon. Its social and political impact can be profound and earth-shaking. To quote Suh Nam-dong again, "The minjung gradually liberate themselves from the position of being a historical object and become a historical subject. Minjung history and theology testify to the fact that the minjung overcome with their own power the external conditions which determine and confine them, and become the subjects who determine their own social situation and destiny."[3]

This is a vision captured by a theologian deeply inspired by the discovery of minjung-people in the Bible, in the traditions of the Christian church, and in the history of his own nation. How is this theological vision to be translated into social and political programs? The question is complex and agonizing, not only for minjung theologians in Korea, but also for liberation theologians in Latin America and in Africa. For Suh Nam-dong at least, that theological vision led him to a deep personal experience of the cross.

A Matter of Emphasis, Not of Substance

The question of revelation and history is both complex and dynamic. There are many stories in the Bible which will help us to appreciate this. The story of the exodus, for instance, is a typical story of the oppressed minjung. Historically, it was a story of the Hebrew slaves making a desperate escape from their oppressors. But how did they come to see it as God's saving act for them? The exodus was the social-political-economic biography of those Hebrew slaves in ancient Egypt. At the same time, it was the biography of their faith. How did that "materialistic" biography become their "spiritual" biography? An unambiguous answer is perhaps difficult. One has to go back to the roots and origins of the Hebrew faith. One may have to apply methods of the history of religions. Whatever the case may be, one may finally have to take account of the "power" not generated by history but at work in history to create change.

The story of the cross and the resurrection is another example. Here again the understanding of the cross and the resurrection in terms of social-political oppression and historical liberation is set in opposition to the theological effort to understand them in relation to salvation. The resurrection of Jesus was no doubt a tremendous experience of liberation on the part of the disciples after their traumatic social-political encounter with the cross of Jesus. But its meaning cannot be totally exhausted by the liberation experienced in the social-political biography of the minjung at the time of Jesus. The resurrection experience in fact expanded that biography into the theology of the reign of God. The cross experience as the social-political biography of minjung acquired, through the resurrection experience, "salvific" meaning not understood when Jesus was executed by the political, and one must add, the religious, authorities. One recalls St. Paul's words: "...we proclaim Christ—yes, Christ nailed to the cross; and though this is a stumbling block to Jews and folly to Greeks, yet to those who have heard his call, Jews and Greeks alike, he is the power of God and the wisdom of God" (1 Cor. 1:23-24). Is it not part of our theological effort to read the social-political-economic biography of the minjung from this post-resurrection insight of Paul? Our effort to be true to the "materialistic" reading of minjung biography is inspired in fact by our deepened and deepening experience of salvation disclosed in the life, the cross and the resurrection of Jesus.

What has become evident is that the theological position taken by minjung theologians has no fundamental difference from that of some other Asian theologians in their effort to do theology in their own situations. It is a matter of emphases rather than of substance. Our common effort must be to press for a dynamic interrelatedness between the biography of the minjung and the biography of God enacted in the biography of Jesus. Theological efforts such as this lead us to the discussion of the fascinating beliefs and practices of Shamanism.

A Theological Look at Shamanism

Theology that lays emphasis on the minjung has to turn to theological exploration of Shamanism, the religion of the minjung. This at once ancient and contemporary, archaic and modern, form of the religious life of people should provide clues to people's tenacious will to live in adverse situations and to the potentially powerful role they could play in social and political changes. In Shamanistic beliefs and practices one finds a biography of the minjung telling in ritual dances and songs the social, political and economic analyses minjung theologians do to develop their theological efforts. Suh Kwang-sun David of Ewha Womans University in Seoul and other experts on Shamanism have enabled us to take a theological look at this spiritual as well as sociopolitical underworld.

A stereotyped verdict on Shamanism is that it is nothing more than a superstition, an anachronism in the life of modern society. But the mystery is that it continues to have a strong hold on men and women throughout Asia today caught in the irreversible process of modernization. In Korea it has survived two thousand years against all odds. Hostility from organized religions such as Buddhism and particularly Confucianism (as the religion of the ruling class) may have driven it underground from time to time, but it has not been eradicated from the life of minjung, the oppressed majority. In fact, the more the minjung encounter hostility, the more they retreat into the world of gods and spirits to gain the power to live, to acquire the wisdom to survive, and to envision a world in which all injustices done to them will be vindicated.

There is plenty of naivete in Shamanistic beliefs and practices. Such naivete could lead to personal tragedy and social absurdity. Disease, for example, is believed to be the result, not of physical causes, but of the displeasure of evil spirits. All sorts of taboos are developed to control and restrict the life of people and to instill fear. And the communication that allegedly takes place with the dead when the *kut* (ritual) reaches the height of frenzy is highly questionable, to say the least.

Yet, to dismiss Shamanism as a superstition of the people still captive to primitive psychology and to an unscientific worldview is not to understand it at all. A purely phenomenological assessment of Shamanism can be very misleading. For Shamanism is, at a deeper level, "a faith for the alienated masses."[4] This is a crucial point. It changes radically one's perception of Shamanism. It brings to light that which is hidden deeply in the life of the minjung and in the history of a nation—*han*! The alienated masses are the people of *han*, of that psycho-somatic anguish and pain resulting from unrequited injustices. The people engaging in Shamanistic rituals body, soul and spirit are thus releasing their accumulated *han*! This release of *han* "brings hope to the people living under oppression in a troubled world."[5] Potentialities implicit in that release of *han* can be nerve-racking. How to exploit those potentialities in establishing the biography of minjung from within their inner spirit world and not merely from objective social and political studies and analyses remains one of the urgent tasks of minjung theology. A theology that deals with the minjung as the subject of history has to touch that invisible part of minjung psyche in which their creative social, political and cultural forces lie.

Expressions such as "accumulated *han*" and "release of *han*" prompts a consideration of the *mudang*, practitioner of Shamanism. *Mudang* is a woman who presides over rituals and practices Shamanistic dances. A *mudang*, for all intents and purposes, is a priestess. A man, or her husband, plays a secondary role by providing, for example, musical accompaniment as she goes about her Shamanistic duties. In folk religions such as Shamanism, the wife, and not the husband, takes the lead. She represents the family in offering sacrifices and prayers. She is the mediator between the world of human beings and the world of gods and spirits. In religious matters she is listened to and obeyed in the village community, even though she is of the lowest social status. This has been the case from ancient times to the present.[6]

This is a strange thing in a male-dominated society such as Korea. Does this mean that in the development of human society a matriarchal social system preceded the patriarchal one? Does it tell us that women may somehow by nature be in closer touch with the mystery of the spirit world than men are? Or is it that by mere chance they were able to establish an enclave within a hierarchical society dominated by men and have kept it under their own control? One can speculate endlessly. The fact is that in the practice of Shamanism women are in charge. They are the masters in that carefully defined religious domain. And it is a vital domain of human existence. When they are at their religious duties, they are no longer subjugated wives in the family and despised members of society. They are persons with authority, respected and feared. As they solemnly offer sacrifices to the gods, their sense of self-importance is high. When they say prayers and ask gods for favor for the family and for the village, they are held in awe and expectation by the people; the welfare and destiny of the community depend on them.

Moreover, as they work themselves to the point of ecstatic frenzy, they must be seized with a tremendous sense of liberation: liberation from the men and society that have enslaved them, repressed them, and treated them as non-persons. Their ritual dance is their emancipation dance. Their songs are liberation songs. They seem to be able to mobilize gods and spirits to join them in their ritual dance and songs of liberation. They release their accumulated *han*: *han* of being a women to whom all kinds of injustices are done by men and society; *han* of their helplessness and powerlessness in face of those injustices; in short, *han* of being a women in a male-dominated world.

Minjung theologians in Korea have heard the *han* of the poor and the oppressed as they take up the study of Korean history with the minjung as the subject and as they engage themselves in scientific social and political analysis. They have also begun to hear the accumulated *han* of minjung in folk religions such as Shamanism. But they must not just hear the accumulated *han* of male minjung. They (and most minjung theologians are male!) must also hear the accumulated *han* of female minjung. This is a potentially explosive *han*! This is a powerful *han* that challenges not only male dominated social and political systems but also male-dominated theology and church.

Urgency for minjung theology to turn to the accumulated *han* of women was impressed upon me when I talked to a group of thinking women Christians. They told me that they were attempting to write a history of Christianity in Korea from the perspective of women. What a laudable and timely undertaking! They go out to the countryside with writing pads and cassette recorders to gather stories from old women believers. Their history of the church in Korea will be constructed on stories these women believers may be able to salvage from their memories. It is going to be a most exciting story theology. I gave them my unreserved encouragement. But they asked me anxiously, "Will our story history be a respectable history?" "Respectable to whom?" I asked them. "To male theologians and historians," they answered. I asked again rather heatedly, "Who sets the standard of respectability? The male? Why don't you create your own respectability? Forget about gaining approval and respect from male theologians and historians! Just be yourself and go ahead with your story theology! You must let the whole male world hear what you women folks have fared in your society and in your church. You must do your own minjung theology!"

From the accumulated *han* of women released in Shamanistic rituals and dances to the accumulated *han* of Christian women seeking to be released! How much more minjung theologians still have to hear! Minjung theology has a long but exciting way to go.

The Culture of Minjung

So theology is not just concepts; it is the life of the minjung. Theology is not merely a matter of the head; it is a matter of the heart. It does not deal with statistics, social research, or political planning only; it has also to deal with the sweat, tears, and laughter of the people. Theology must be a body language, "heart semantics," or "soul syntax," to be able to understand statistics and analytical data, to grasp and experience the pain and suffering of the minjung, and to reconstruct culture already richly embedded in the life and history of the minjung.

If history must be reevaluated and rewritten on the basis of the biography of the minjung, culture too must be reconstructed as culture of the minjung. The culture that expresses the life, thought, and activity of a people and a nation has been very elitist in form and content. It is almost synonymous with sophisticated life, high education, cultivated manners, expensive tastes in food, dress, or interior decoration. Culture is what you will find in the courts of kings and rulers. It is what you will see in an opera house or in an art gallery. If this is truly what culture is, then slum-dwellers have no culture. The poor do not possess it. Nor do the oppressed have the freedom to create culture. If this is what culture is, then culture, to the minjung, is a symbol and reality of oppression.

But the truth of the matter is that minjung do have culture. They create culture out of the life of misery. They make culture as they struggle to live in this hostile world and to make sense of this senseless life. The biography of the minjung is the biography of their culture. Folk music, folk dance, folk drama, folk story, without which no national culture is complete, have their foundations in ritual dances, songs and dramas associated with Shamanism practiced by *mudangs* from the despised and oppressed members of society!

On a lucky day called "House Day" in the Tenth Month of the year, for example, cakes and wine made from newly harvested grains are offered to the spirits of the house in order to gain peace and happiness. The *mudang*, invited to conduct the ritual, dances and chants the prayer:

> On dragon's day the foundation is made;
> On crane's heads the cornerstones are laid;
> And with golden tiles and jade stones is built
> Ah, pretty house!
> At the corners of the caves wind-bells hang,
> And, when the southeast wind blows,
> Ah, pretty music!
> The master of this house,
> His body purified in clear water,
> He offers before thee,
> Oh Spirit of the House!
> Since he prays thee with heart and soul,
> Help thyself with good appetite.
> Bring more wealth to this house.
> Fulfill all its wishes.
> Let no ill-health visit here;
> Let no evil spirit approach near;
> I pray thee, protect this house by thy radiant power![7]

Too worldly a prayer to be of theological significance? Perhaps. But for most people religion begins with worldly concerns. For them the body is the medium of the spirit. Christian theology has to reckon with this "bodily" reality of people's faith.

There is beauty in this prayer. "When the southeast wind blows, ah pretty music!" One hears music in the wind. It is a music praising the beautiful autumn day. The music carries the fragrance of the colors that adorn trees and flowers. It prays to the gods for golden harvests in the fields. And it makes the wish that the community be sustained in peace and well-being. Reflected in the beauty of the prayer is the sincere faith in "the radiant power" of the deity venerated and placated. It is such faith that enables the minjung to contain *han* in their souls and bodies. It is the same faith that makes it possible for them to endure their accumulated *han* until the moment of truth, the moment when *han*, under intolerable social, political and economic pressures, bursts their bodies and souls to become a mighty force that changes the course of history.

Minjung, the subject of history but the object of oppression, not only gain the strength and hope to live from their empathy with nature, but also show their moral power in their empathy with those, like themselves, subjected to injustice. One of the folk songs sung on "the Cold Food Day" in the Second Moon or the Third Moon when ancestors are remembered at the graveyard is as heart-rending as it is moving:

> Second moon came and cold food I eat.
> Far over the mountain spring buds are out,
> Withered trees revive and faded flowers bloom.
> Yea, his memory reflects in my heart,
> But a man once gone comes back no more;
> My hot tears drop on this cold food,
> Even this cold food I offer on thy grave
> For your hungry soul to partake.
> Butterflies dance with heavy wings.
> With heavy heart I bathe in the icy water
> And sit by the stream to sing to thy memory.
> Lo, the mountains turn pink and azaleas laugh,
> Willow branches wave green in the breeze
> Like the hair of a maiden of sixteen.
> The farmers take plough to the fields
> And the herd boys astride their pets
> Raise golden whips to catch the spring.

A marvelous interweaving of the biography of humanity and the biography of nature! And there is a story of an infinite *han* that brings the past and the present, the dead and the living, to the mourners' loud cry of "Aigo! Aigo!" at the ancestral gravesite each Second or Third Moon of the year.

The story that lives on in the memory of the people and is echoed far and near both in time and in space is this:

> Long, long ago in China in the Kingdom of Chin there lived a loyal subject named Chu Kai-ja. The treacherous retainers hated him and drove him out of the king's presence.
> Poor Chu Kai-ja then ran far away and hid himself in a mountain called Chinshan.... The king heard this, and, as he admired the steadfast loyalty of Chu Kai-ja, searched for him throughout the kingdom, but without success. At last it was learned that he was hiding in a cave in the mountain and, in order to force him out, they set fire to the forest.

He did not come out, but remained hiding and was suffo-
cated to death. Out of pity and admiration for his staunch
fidelity, all the people throughout the country refrained
from making fire to cook their food and ate only cold things
in memory of his sad end. In due course this custom was
brought to Korea.[8]

Historical roots of folk things run deep in the life and history of a
people. The folk song sung at the graveyard at the present time
and the story of the wronged loyal minister in the ancient time become blended in the consciousness of the people as they mourn
their ancestors and remind themselves of injustices in their society. One may call this "culture of *han*." Its theological impact on
Christians and theologians are powerful and profound. Is it not
then the task of minjung theologians to help build a theological
culture of minjung, bringing to light the *han* of the people sub-
merged in the consciousness of the national psyche?

Dance of *Han*
Usually, minjung culture is an internalized culture. In oppressive
situations people learn to hide their feelings. Living under a repressive social and political system, men and women have to suppress their anger and sorrow. They have to "swallow their tears
into their stomachs." They do not put into sophisticated words a
deep sense of injustice boiling in their bowels. They do not use
elaborate art forms to vent the anger gnawing their souls. And
they do not refine their sorrow into a euphemism that reduces the
harsh realities of life to a passing sentimentalism.

But there are times when their long suppressed anger and sorrow
erupt volcano-like out of the abyss of their being in fury and frenzy.
Then there are protests, revolts, or revolutions. There are also ways
in which the pain and suffering they endure in silence get translated into plays, dramas, dances and songs. These folk art forms are
raw, spontaneous and unsophisticated. They are direct, powerful
and explosive. They expose the heart of a culture that is noble, true
and beautiful, revealing how men, women and children in their
poverty, wretchedness and helplessness strive to be human.

Some of us who have explored the subject of theological culture
of the minjung have seen a minjung culture in action in its rawest
form, in its most powerful expression, and in its astonishing virtuo-

so performance. One such opportunity I have had was watching a solo musical called "Soo Goong Ga" (Song of the Water Palace) performed by a woman artist, Kong Ok-jin for the men and women who packed the small Space Theatre in Seoul one fall evening in 1983.

The musical was based on a folktale of a turtle on a mission to secure a hare liver said to be able to heal the acute pain that had developed in the stomach of the Dragon King of the water palace at the bottom of the sea. The turtle found a hare and was able to induce it to the water palace to be slaughtered for its liver. But the clever hare did not lose its wits at that critical moment of its life. It duped the Dragon King and the whole court of sea creatures into believing that it had left its liver on the land and had the turtle dutifully bring it back to the shore. After it was safely out of danger, the hare said to the outwitted turtle:

> What a turtle you are! Now I can understand the phrase "as foolish as a turtle." Do you still believe that I can pull out and push back my liver like a toy? I only fooled your Dragon King and his whole court in the hour of my imminent danger. After all, the malady of your Dragon King has nothing to do with me. You kidnapped me with a fine trick in order to live yourself more happily at the cost of my life. So I feel very much like killing you, but, considering your good service in carrying me to and from the water palace through winds and waves, I pardon your crime and spare your remaining life. Now you go back and tell your Dragon King to forget my liver, and kiss death with a glad heart, for no medicine can insure an immortal life or resist death, which embraces a prince or a peasant as equals when the zero hour comes.[9]

This is a fascinating folk tale. One can explore it with endless theological fascination. A rich political culture of minjung is embedded in it.

Kong Ok-jin was a diminutive woman of fifty, frail looking and unassuming. As she began her dance to the accompaniment of the music played on Korean traditional instruments, she became transformed. She was no longer a frail looking woman, but a little dynamo ready to explode herself and the audience with her most "primitive" energy of creation. As the dance progressed, she became soaked in the sweat freely exuding from her body. She was totally immersed in her dance. Her entire being was the dance.

The dance was her entire being. She could not be distinguished from her dance, nor the dance from her. She was no longer a woman of fifty. She was a girl in her early twenties, nimble, supple, and dynamic. I had never seen a dance with such convincing power of the body, the heart, and the spirit united in the ecstasy of a being in communion with the transcendent power—the power invoked to redress injustices, to right wrongs, to bless the helpless and to empower the powerless. This is a Shamanistic dance! This is a *mudang* dance! The audience was spellbound. They became enraptured in a culture of the spirit world carefully secluded in the depths of their humanity but now bursting into the open. This was at once an awesome and liberating experience.

She was the Dragon King with an acute pain in the stomach. Her face contorted in anguish. Her body writhed in agony. Though in pain, the Dragon King was still the king with an absolute power over his subjects. She was now the queen, the princes and the princesses knitting their brows and clasping their hands in vain effort to assuage the king's pain. Then she was cuttlefish, the physician, attending the king in fear and trembling, knowing that with its failure to cure the king it would forfeit life as well. And she was those small and large fishes tiptoeing in grim faces, more worried about their fate than the king's malady, should something happen to their king.

Then there was this turtle on the "mission impossible" to entice a hare to the water palace. She was now that turtle, crawling on the floor. And when the hare was found at last, she was that hare jumping up and down the cliffs by the sea. When the hare was brought to the water palace, she was all these creatures in rapid succession—the Dragon King in pain, cuttlefish the physician administering medicine, the turtle a little proud of the mission accomplished, and the hare fascinated at first by marvels of the undersea world but quickly seized with fear when it saw the fate awaiting it. Then, there was the long voyage of the turtle back to the shore with the hare on its back. Finally, she was the hare standing tall on a rock, obviously relieved and elated by its narrow escape from the water palace, venting its undisguised contempt for the Dragon King who sought to gain immortality at the expense of the innocent and unsuspecting creatures such as the hare. And there she was at once the turtle again, stupefied, still trying to figure out what happened.

How did she become such an artist with such a gripping power over her audience? How did she learn those movements of the body and the expressions of the face to make visible the invisible reality normally hidden in the subconscious realm of human existence? Such questions led to the story of her life with her deaf-mute younger brother in a poverty-stricken home.[10]

Desperately trying to amuse her brother, she twisted her face and contorted her body until she was able to induce a smile from him. In an effort to reach that part of her brother's humanity cruelly disabled by the incapacitated sense organs she did not spare herself until she was able to communicate with him with body language. She must have been in despair often. She must have wanted to give up in desperation more than once. She must have cried her heart out when her efforts seemed futile, unable to penetrate that sometimes blank and often silly-looking exterior of her brother and get nearer to his heart which, she believed, must be as sensitive, expectant and responsive as hers.

Without knowing it, she was doing dance of *han* in front of her crippled brother. She was perfecting that art of hers that enables her to reach out into the souls of those afflicted in body and in spirit. She became a *mudang* of *han* dance as she struggled to create a communion of hearts and souls with her severely disabled brother.

One of the many encores she did that night—she seemed unlimited in her repertoire as well as in her energy—was the dance of a mentally retarded person. In her dance she was the mentally retarded person. She tried to unbear her heart barred by the body and the mind, and damaged by the terrible deformity. She tottered. She fell. She strove to rise again. Her effort to smile turned into a hideous grimace. Her attempt to form words only resulted in a hissing sound. And her longing for human communication made her seem even more ridiculous and repulsive. She was enacting the pain of a mentally retarded person. She was speaking with her body the anguish of all the physically and mentally disabled persons. And she did succeed in letting their humanity break out of their pain and suffering. Here was the dance of *han*. And here was the dance of hope.

The folk culture represented by Kong Ok-jin was a great tribute to her mastery of the body art of dance. Even more, it was a great testimony to the inner vitality imprisoned in the suppressed humanity of the minjung. A wide horizon of minjung culture loomed large for minjung theology that night in the Space Theatre of Seoul. People's stories, poetry, music, dance—theological mastery of these arts is indispensable to hearing the genuine cry of the people from the depths of their injured humanity. To explore them theologically is to be in touch with that human spiritual power that moves history and changes its course, that strives to be free from shackles of dehumanization.

Shaking hands with her and thanking her for her consummate artistry, I saw her face still aglow with the fire she had kindled in the womb of minjung humanity. Her entire body was still radiating the heat of hope generated out of her struggle with despair. That night she overwhelmed us with that fire and overpowered us with that heat. Can minjung theology also be aglow with that fire of minjung humanity? Will it radiate that heat that empowers people in their struggle for justice, freedom and love?

Notes

1. Suh Nam-dong, "In Search of Minjung Theology, " tr. from Korean by Suh Kwang-sun David in his paper "Called to Witness to the Gospel Today—The Priesthood of *Han*," read at the consultation on the "Called to Witness" study held in Seoul, September 19-20, 1984. The consultation was held under the auspices of the World Alliance of Reformed Churches in connection with the centennial celebrations of the churches in Korea.

2. See, for example, Kim Yong-bock's essay, "Messiah and Minjung: Discerning Messianic Politics over against Political Messianism," *Minjung Theology: People as the Subjects of History*, pp. 185-196.

3. Suh Nam-dong, "Historical References for a Theology of Minjung," *Minjung Theology*, p. 170.

4. Ryu Tong-shik, "Shamanism: The Dominant Folk Religion in Asia," read at the Inter-religious Conference held at Tao Fong Shan Ecumenical Center, Hong Kong, September 13-17, 1983.

5. Ryu Tong-shik, "Shamanism," p. 11.

6. See Chang Yu-shik, "Shamanism as Folk Existentialism," *Religion in Korea*, eds. Earl H. Philips and Yu Eui-young. (Los Angeles: Centre for Korean-American and Korean Studies, 1982).

7. See Ha Tae-hung, *Folk Customs and Family Life* (Seoul: Yonsei University Press, 1958), pp. 53-54.

8. For the story and the poem, see Ha Tae-hung, *Folk Cultures and Family Life*, pp. 27-28.

9. The story in its entirety is to be found in Ha Tae-hung, *Folk Tales of Old Korea* (Seoul: Yonsei University Press, 1958), pp. 50-57.

10. Hyun Yong-hak tells Kong Ok-jin's story in his unpublished paper "Crippled Beggar's Dance."

Food is Heaven

(From Kim Chi Ha's writing on *Chang Il-dam*, translated by Jung Young Lee)

Food is heaven.
Food cannot be made alone.
Food is to be shared.
Food is heaven.

Everyone sees
The same stars in the sky.
It is natural that
Everyone shares the same food.

Food is heaven.
When we eat,
God comes in and
Dwells in us.
Food is heaven.

Oh, Food should be shared
By all of us.

"Building the House by Righteousness": The Ecumenical Horizons of Minjung Theology

by Kosuke Koyama

Woe to him who builds his house by unrighteousness, and his upper rooms by injustice; who makes his neighbor serve him for nothing, and does not give him his wages....Did not your father eat and drink and do justice and righteousness? Then it was well with him. He judged the cause of the poor and needy; then it was well. Is not this to know me? says the Lord. But you have eyes and heart only for your dishonest gain, for shedding innocent blood, and for practicing oppression and violence (Jeremiah 22:13-17).

These words of God that Jeremiah delivers against the king Jehoiakim who "builds his house by unrighteousness" (through demolishing people's human rights) express the spirit of the Korean minjung theology. Because of his critical words addressed to those who ignore the ethical commandments of God and exploit the people (minjung), Jeremiah was arrested and imprisoned. Since 1970, the Korean minjung theologians are also expelled from their academic and ecclesiastical positions, are endlessly interrogated by the "topdogs" (a term suggested by Hyun Young-hak) who do not judge "the cause of the poor and needy," and are frequently imprisoned.

Korean minjung theology belongs to the honored tradition of Christian prison theology. During the last fifteen years, prison experience and Christian theology have found sacramental union in the story of minjung theology. "Why have we been fighting against the Park regime [Park Chong-hee]? For human liberation; to recover the humanity God gave us; to be free people. Nothing is more important. We must press ahead," says Kim Chi Ha's letter from Seoul's West Gate prison (*The Gold-Crowned Jesus and Other Writings* [Maryknoll, N.Y.: Orbis Books, 1978], p. 37). Altogether,

Kim Chi Ha spent 12 years in prison for his opposition to South Korea's dictatorial government.

Jeremiah's words are irritating to those who force their neighbors to serve them for nothing—whether they be individuals, members of a group, or the powerful elite of a nation or an empire. The God of Jeremiah abhors dishonest gain, shedding of innocent blood, and the practice of oppression and violence. This God is the message of Korean minjung theology. Minjung theology is a restatement and reenactment of the ancient biblical tradition. It takes its orders, to borrow a phrase from Bishop Desmond Tutu, neither from Washington nor Moscow, but from Galilee. "Christ lived, and died" writes Kim Dae-jung, the renowned leader of the opposition to the South Korean regime, "for those whose natural rights were suppressed. Therefore, to be a Christian is to fight on behalf of the oppressed and to make necessary sacrifices" ("Christianity, Human Rights and Democracy in Korea," an address given at Emory University, March 31, 1983).

Minjung theology is convinced, as deeply as Jeremiah was, that the suppression of human rights and the practice of exploitation cannot be compatible with "knowing God." Minjung theology affirms the unity of "theological beholding" (Behold, the Lamb of God, who takes away the sin of the world!) and "ethical walking" ("to do justice, and to love kindness, and to walk humbly with your God"). This unity is the heart of minjung theology. About the beginning of this theological movement, Moon Hee-suk Cyris writes:

> Since 1970, theologians in Korea have been confronted with a different theological agenda. In the streets and university campuses ordinary people, intellectuals, laborers and even poets have begun to proclaim the message of the Bible in ways that are relevant to the current economic-socio-political context of Korea. In this situation, scholars have been challenged to provide a biblical perspective for understanding the reality of the minjung (people)—those who are politically oppressed, impoverished, and subjected to insult and contempt" ("An Old Testament Understanding of Minjung," *Minjung Theology* [Maryknoll, N.Y., London, Singapore: Orbis Books, Zed, CCA, 1983], p. 123).

Faith in the biblical God is incongruous with letting the people live in subjection to insult and contempt. Positing the Korean cultural sentiment of *han* (a deep feeling of unresolved resentment against unjustifiable suffering—see Jung Young Lee's description, p. 8) to be the central value in construction of Korean Christian theology, Suh Nam-dong writes: "If one does not hear the sighs of the *han* of the minjung, one cannot hear the voice of Christ knocking on our doors." According to Suh Nam-dong the most important thesis of Kim Chi Ha's minjung theology is "the unification of God and revolution." Suh Kwang-sun David writes that minjung theology provides "a framework of political theology which takes into consideration the socioeconomic and political history of Korea and the sociopolitical biography of the Christian koinonia in Korea." These expressions point to the union of "theological beholding" and "ethical walking."

Such a vibrant theological movement cannot be called by one name only. It may be spoken of in a number of ways: a theology in the Korean interrogation room; a Korean prison theology; a theology of costly discipleship; a theology of dialogue with destitutes and prostitutes; a theology between the underdog and the topdog; a theology intersecting Korean culture and social concerns; a theology of proclamation-preaching; a theology of social justice in the perspective of the Lord's Supper; a theology of politics of God; and so on. The Christian commitment and passion that cuts through all these theological reflections and actions is the conviction that "to know God" (theological beholding) means concretely to stop building the house through unrighteousness (ethical walking). This is the theme of minjung theology. The theme suggests expanding ecumenical horizons and corresponding theological challenges, "for this was not done in a corner" (Acts 26:26).

The Ecumenical Significance of Minjung Theology
There are three relevant questions related to minjung theology which must be asked: What is the ecumenical meaning of the concepts presented by minjung theology in the areas of eschatology, conflict and culture?

Eschatology
Reflection upon the nature of the religious life of humanity may suggest to us two types of universality: cosmological and eschatological. The cosmologically defined universality is to be understood in relation to heaven and earth. It is a natural universality,

salvific in an all-embracing way (Mother Earth, Father Heaven). None of us lives outside "heaven and earth." I may characterize the nature of this universality by changing a few words of the famous verse of Psalm 139 to read: "If I ascend to heaven, heaven is there! If I make my bed in Sheol, earth is there!" This reveals a nature orientation.

The eschatologically defined universality, on the other hand, is that of "the maker of heaven and earth" (Psalm 121:2). It is not a "natural" universality. It contains the element of transcendence since it speaks of One who is beyond heaven and earth. While the universality of heaven and earth gives us security because it is predictable (the sun rises in the east every morning with dependable regularity), the universality of the maker of heaven and earth does not give us such an immediate sense of security. The maker is not predictable in the way heaven and earth are. "If I ascend to heaven, thou art there! If I make my bed in Sheol, thou art there!" This suggests a history orientation. The eschatological universality confronts us while the cosmological universality embraces us. The Semitic faiths ("the children of Abraham," i.e., Judaism, Christianity and Islam) hold to an eschatological universality. The Hindu and Chinese religious world of the East understands the cosmological universality. In both traditions the concept of universality is central to their doctrines of salvation. Both intimate that salvation, in order to be salvation, must be found in the context of some kind of universality.

It is parochial to say that a system of social ethics is to be found only in the context of eschatological universality, as though it were impossible for the cosmological orientation to conceive of a social ethic. The cosmological mind finds its highest social-ethical value in a harmonious cosmic totality (equilibrium). Generally, the "emperor" stands at the axis of this totality as a person representing the cosmic movement that brings benefit to humanity. In the Japan of recent history (up to 1945) we see a fanatical form of this cosmological politics, centered in the literal divinity of the emperor. The weakness of the cosmological social ethic is its lack of a principle of criticism against the imperial power. This ancient form of cosmological politics is so deeply rooted in the human mind and is still so pervasive in the world of political symbolism that we cannot afford to overlook it.

The Semitic tradition of "the maker of heaven and earth" has

given humanity a socioethical insight that is deeply concerned
with history. It contains the principle of transcendence by which
the imperial power can be criticized. "The kings of the earth set
themselves...against the Lord....He who sits in the heavens
laughs" (Psalm 2:1-4). "Thus says the Lord to his anointed, to Cyr-
us..." (Isaiah 45:1). It is by this eschatological social ethics that
King Jehoiakim was criticized. And it is this tradition which has
been given voice in Korean minjung theology.

Korea belongs to the spiritual tradition of the East. Cosmological universality is a part of her cultural life. Yet, more than any
Asian people (including the Christian Filipinos!), the Koreans
seem also to have appropriated into their religious orientation
the message of the eschatological universality. This is a characteristic of the Korean people that puzzles other Asians. There
have been a number of messianic movements in both Korea and Japan in the last two hundred years, but those of Korea exhibit a
stronger sense of history than do those of Japan.

The people of Korea have understood the historical meaning of
"conversion" (discontinuity and radical reorientation) as enunciat-
ed by the prophets of the Hebrew Scriptures far better than have
other Asians. Chon Kyon-mo is correct in saying that the Koreans
understand the biblical concept of person in the presence of a holy
God in a way that the Japanese, who accomplished "modernization" on the basis of pagan anthropology, do not (Sekai, February
1979, pp. 143-156). The secret for this "Calvinism of Korea" must
be, in my view, that her historical experience of suffering has giv-
en her a more mature understanding of the meaning of history.
How mature Korean thought has been in this respect can be appre-
ciated when we see that the naturalistic cosmological doctrine of
salvation has not been rejected outright. It has been preserved,
though subordinated to the eschatological perspective.

The universality of minjung theology has been constructed upon
the rich heritage of the biblical theological structure in which
the cosmological is subordinated to the eschatological. Hyun
Young-hak hints characteristically of this theological structure
in his chapter, "A Theological Look at the Mask Dance in Korea,"
(Minjung Theology, pp. 47-54). "The mask dance is composed," he
writes, "not only of dance but also rhythmic instrumental music,
songs and dialogue between the performers and the musicians and
between the performers and the audience.... The mask dance is full

of humor, satire and vulgar expressions with a great deal of sex-related dirty words" (p. 47).

The description points to the presence of cosmological emotion as a primary cultural background to such dance performance. Using this indirect form of mask dance, according to Hyun Young-hak, the minjung say what Jeremiah said to the powerful rulers. The cosmological is fundamentally sexual (therefore the "sex-related dirty words"). Cosmological sexuality gives the language, dance and music through which the eschatological ("do not build the house by unrighteousness!") is pronounced. "Mask" is a symbol in which serious messages are efficiently communicated through "dirty words."

Hyun Young-hak calls this dialectical arrangement "critical transcendence." He comments, "In and through the mask dance, the minjung, the ordinary folks, experience and express a critical transcendence over this world and laugh at its absurdity. By satirizing the aristocrats they stand over against the aristocrats. By laughing at the old monk they stand above him" (p. 50).

In his article "Towards a Theology of *Han*" (*Minjung Theology*, pp. 55-69), Suh Nam-dong makes a dramatic use of the cosmological to express the eschatological. He introduces Yang Sung-woo's concept of *han* as found in his *Slave Diary*. The *han* "which has been absorbed into the bones and muscles of the people of the country for 5,000 years is still breathing in the roots of the grass which covers the graves of the dead" (p. 62).

The Korean *han* corresponds to Japanese *urami*. *Urami* is a characteristic property of the unpacified spirit of the deceased. Such an unpacified spirit is called *onryo* (*urami*-spirit). The *onryo* are feared among the Japanese people for their power to take revenge upon the living. This they are particularly likely to wreak upon those who destroyed them by throwing their lives, in turn, into havoc. The *onryo* is a *urami* spirit disturbed by its cosmological homelessness.

The Japanese have not utilized the energy of the *onryo* to achieve social ethical values. They have been preoccupied with pacifying the *onryo* through cosmological rituals. Thus the dimension of social ethics is lacking in the Japanese *onryo* doctrine. In contrast, Suh Nam-dong introduces Kim Chi Ha's notion that "*han* can be sublimated in dynamic form as the energy for revolution." Kim Chi Ha speaks about *dan* (cutting) of the vicious continuity of *han*:

Cutting the chain of the circulation of *han—dan* is for the transformation of the secular world and secular attachments, accumulated *han* being met with continuous *dan*. On the one hand, there is the fearful *han* which can kill, cause revenge, destroy and hate endlessly, and on the other, there is the repetition of *dan* to suppress the explosion which can break out of the vicious circle, so that *han* can be sublimated as higher spiritual power. The opening of the total dimension of the minjung with a dialectical unification of the complicated *han* and *dan*; that is the decisive basis of my artistic effort. *Dan* is to overcome *han*. Personally, it is self-denial. Collectively, it is to cut the vicious circle of revenge" (pp. 64-65).

Here we find a transformation of the energy of *han* to social ethics. Through *dan, han* becomes a social value. It is not simply *han*, but *han* which is "cut" (*dan*) and proclaims, "do not build the house by unrighteousness."

Hyun Young-hak, Suh Nam-dong, and Kim Chi Ha thus demonstrate their art of mobilizing the cosmological in order to express the eschatological. Classic examples of the same art are found in the teaching of Jesus, "What father among you, if his son asks for a fish, will instead of a fish give him a serpent?...How much more will the heavenly Father give the Holy Spirit to those who ask him!" (Lk. 11:11-13) That which is natural, predictable, and cosmological is mobilized to express that which is of grace, unpredictable and eschatological. But this mobilization depends upon faith in One who is beyond heaven and earth. "If God so clothes the grass of the field, which today is alive and tomorrow is thrown into the oven, will he not much more clothe you, O men of little faith?" (Matt. 6:30)

These three minjung theologians, theologizing among the minjung of Korea, prefer that it is not they, but the minjung themselves who say in their own terms that it is "God who clothes the grass of the field." The missiological significance of this sensitivity cannot be overemphasized. The "universality" in Christian theology must not be an imperialistic concept. It must have the wisdom to make use of the cosmological in order to express the eschatological, and to wait for the minjung to express the primacy of God in history in their own terms.

Conflict

The three Semitic faiths (Judaism, Christianity, Islam) condemn "building the house by unrighteousness." The teaching of the two great sages of Asia, the Buddha and Confucius, equally stand with Jeremiah in this protest. In this, Korean minjung theology has the full support of all the great ancient spiritual traditions of humanity and is positively congruous with the enduring ecumenical consensus of those traditions. The universal creed is to "build the house with righteousness!"

The oppressors of the minjung are those who hold power. Who are the oppressed minjung? Hyun Young-hak declares:

> We think of the poor peasants who are squeezed out of the farm, young industrial workers who are forced to work under inhuman conditions, the inner city poor who are struggling to survive in squatters' areas under the ever present threat of eviction; day laborers, peddlers, hawkers, swindlers, junk collectors, rag and waste paper collectors, hoodlums, prostitutes, pimps, sorcerers, shamans, fortunetellers, cheap wine sellers, and bargirls (Public Lecture at Union Theological Seminary, New York, April 13, 1982).

Exploitation and oppression have been practiced overtly and crassly as well as subtly and in sophisticated, hidden ways. Tragically, the oppressed are commonly manipulated to serve the powerful in their own exploitation. One does not have to be a Marxist to observe that the powerful oppress the weak. Exploitation has been a mark of the human condition throughout history.

What is new in our world is the way in which advancements in the technology of communications and transportation have made it possible for powerful interests to extend their influence internationally. The scale of oppression has become global. Power has been consolidated in board rooms and military establishments until its crushing weight seems certain to destroy the powerless. Yet the oppressed are preserved as their exploitation is essential to the diabolical scheme of greed which has gripped our world. Thus two ecumenisms, an ecumenism against greed, heralded by the great religious traditions of humanity, and an ecumenism of greed, fostered by corporations and military establishments, are in conflict. Humanity has its existence in the context of this conflict. Yet the disturbing truth is that these two ecumenisms are confusedly intertwined, and are becoming increasingly more so. Jesus' well-known parable speaks to this painful reality in our history: "'Then do you want us to go and gather them?' But he said, 'No; lest in gathering the weeds you root up the wheat along with them. Let both grow together until the harvest; and at harvest time I will tell the reapers. Gather the weeds first and bind them in bundles to be burned, but gather the wheat into my barn'" (Matt. 13:28-30).

The painful truth of our human condition is that "Elijah" and "the prophets of the Baal" (I Kings 18) are far more complicit, particularly in today's rapidly changing technological and economic world, than we would like to believe. There is no "clean" money in circulation in the world today when astronomical amounts of money are allocated to military budgets and equally stupendous sums are controlled by a few giant corporations. It is impossible for the "Elijahs" (Christian ministers and theological professors) not to be entangled with the money touched by the "Baal."

When he destroyed the prophets of Baal (450 of them!) at the brook Kishon, Elijah committed a sin of overkill. He overstepped the human limitation that prohibits the pronouncement of judgment "before the time" (I Cor. 4:5). ("Judge not, that you be not judged" [Matt. 7:1]. "For the wrath of God is revealed from heaven against all ungodliness..." (Rom. 1:18). Elijah became so jealous of God that he could not leave the "Last Judgment" eschatologically in the hand of God alone. The concept of the two ecumenisms contains the painful ambiguity of history which awaits eagerly for the eschatological moment in which the separation between sheep and goats will take place (Matt. 25:31-32). Christian ecumenism cannot free itself from this eschatological tension.

It is, however, in this very expectation of the eschatological moment that minjung theology says that to "know God" is to oppose "building the house by unrighteousness," now, in the concrete context of everyday life today. By uniting theological beholding and ethical walking minjung theology unpacks the critical significance of eschatology. For Christian eschatology sees that even though the possibility of the Last Judgment lies in God alone (theological beholding), at the same time it is our responsibility to approximate the Last Judgment in this world by staging our opposition against evil (ethical walking). Suh Nam-dong's distinction between the symbols of the Kingdom of God and millennium is important in this juncture:

While the Kingdom of God is a heavenly and ultimate symbol, the millennium is a historical, earthly and semi-
ultimate symbol. Accordingly, the Kingdom of God is understood as the place the believer enters when he dies, but the
millennium is understood as the point at which history and
society are renewed. Therefore, in the Kingdom of God the
salvation of the individual person is secured, but in the millennium is secured the salvation of the whole social reality of
humankind. Consequently, while the Kingdom of God is used
in the ideology of the ruler, the millennium is the symbol of
the aspiration of the minjung (*Minjung Theology*, pp. 162-163).

My response to this is that unfortunately the church, as Suh Nam-
dong indicates, misinterpreted the dynamic symbol of the Kingdom of God demonstrated in the life of Jesus. "If it is by the finger
of God that I cast out demons, then the kingdom of God has come
upon you" (Luke 11:20). The kingdom of God is to do with the unexpected manifestation of the power of God in this world of ours, not
the place the believer enters at death.

The theological word "eschatology" usually connotes something that happens in the "future." The richness of the Christian
eschatology is found, however, in discovering the eschatological
moments (the surprise coming of the transcendent God into our history) in the past, present, and future. The tradition of faith affirms, to quote Martin Luther, this free "visitation of God." Eschatology as the visitation of God created Christian sacraments
within the context of our everyday life. At the visitation of God
our time is sacramentalized. "Do this in remembrance of me" (I
Cor. 11:24). In remembering Christ at the Last Supper, our past,
present, and future are saved from fragmentation and disintegra-
tion. According to minjung theology, this moment of "making the
time sacred" occurs when "worldly food (bread) and heavenly
food (freedom)" are united.

The God who has visited us is the God who will visit us. The
visitation of God is reenacted when we remember the sacred event
that took place on the night he was betrayed. That sacred event
cannot be separated from the history that brought about the be-
trayal. So, also, "in remembrance of me" includes remembering the
history of the world. The history of Christ and the history of people must be remembered together. The history of "building the

house with unrighteousness" must be remembered if we are to learn the skills of building a righteous house. Unless the two are held together in our thought, Christian discipleship will become romantic, irresponsible, and ineffective. "The true light that enlightens every man was coming into the world" (John 1:9). The name of Christ contains the world's history (Rev. 21:6).

In the symbol of the Kingdom of God, the history of Christ and the history of the world intersect. The Korean minjung theologians remember both histories, and that is the way, according to them, that the painful past is brought to Christ's healing presence. They have provided us with a signpost toward a Christian understanding of conflict in the ecumenical experience of humanity today.

The story of the relationship between the peoples of the Japanese archipelago and the Korean peninsula has been one of the massive perpetration of injury upon the Koreans by the Japanese. Throughout the history of the two countries Korea has never invaded Japan. Through Korea, the ancient, backward Japan received many cultural gifts. Yet, from ancient times, the Japanese have looked upon the Koreans with contempt and treated them with bellicosity. Japanese aggression culminated in the colonization of Korea from 1910 to 1945. The "treaty" of August 22, 1910, forced upon Korea by an overpowering military threat and negotiated through large-scale bribery of the Korean ruling class, reads, "His Majesty the Emperor of Korea makes the complete and permanent cession to His Majesty the Emperor of Japan of all rights of sovereignty over the whole of Korea." For thirty-five years Korea was administered by nine Japanese Governor Generals in succession, all of military background. That the Governor General must be a military man was stipulated in the Imperial Command, No. 354, article 2, issued in 1910.

It would be too much to recite here the endless atrocities of the Japanese during the thirty-five years of colonial dominance over the people of Korea. The day Japan surrendered to the Allied Powers (August 15, 1945) was a day of emancipation, a day of "exodus" for the Korean people from the land of slavery. Jubilation engulfed the cities and villages of Korea.

Unfortunately, the Japanese people quickly forgot what they had done to Korea. The official position of the Japanese government for the last forty years has been to defend its colonial rule over Korea, claiming that it brought more benefit to Korea than injury. In November 1963, Japan honored Hirobumi Ito, the Meiji architect of imperial Japan, despised by every Korean, by placing his image on the Japanese one thousand yen paper currency!

In the summer of 1982, a dispute over "History Textbook Revision" spread quickly throughout Asian capitals. Asian countries that suffered under Japanese occupation during the war years demanded that Japanese history textbooks for school children tell the truth about the war and state plainly, for instance, that the Japanese army "invaded" (*shinryaku*) China, instead of saying that the Japanese army "advanced" (*shinshutsu*) into China.

On August 5, 1982, the Ministry of Education of the Republic of Korea published a document of 20,000 words demonstrating the willful distortion of the Korean image in Japanese publications from ancient times to the present; e.g., the Japanese government "recommended" (instead of "forced") the Koreans to worship at Shinto shrines; the Koreans were "left free" to speak Japanese, while in truth they were "forced" to do so. The Japanese emperor callously ignored that document when, on the occasion of the state visit to Japan of the Korean President, Chun Doo-hwan, in September 1983, he spoke, in his official speech of welcome, of the colonial days merely as an "unfortunate past" (September 7, 1983). The nation that had victimized her neighbors easily forgot what it had done. The Japanese people live in carefree ignorance of the enormous pain their own country inflicted upon Korea. In minjung theology, however, the Korean experience under the Japanese rule has been integrated into the people's total historical experience.

Minjung theology does not see history as a stage on which the struggle between good and evil takes place as does Persian religious thought. What concern the minjung theologians are historical experiences and historical stories, such as how the Japanese Governor Generals ruled Korea through the ubiquitous Special Police Branch. They call attention to the unconsolable lamentation of the relatives of the hundreds of Koreans who, conscripted to work in military factories in Hiroshima, perished in that fateful city in August 1945. During the war years, thousands of Korean women were mobilized to the "patriotic" duty of "comforting troops." All these historical stories, not speculations about the metaphysical principles of good and evil, are taken seriously in their "contextual" theology.

Since minjung theology understands the conflict between the oppressor and the oppressed historically rather than metaphysically, it is free from the metaphysical "ideology of conflict." When it opted for "stories" rather than "metaphysics," minjung theology took a harder path. History is always more painful and confusing than metaphysics. Jeremiah's agonizing words express the honest human puzzlement about history: "Why does the way of the wicked prosper? Why do all who are treacherous thrive?" (12:2). Why is it that God "protects Cain" (Genesis 4:15)? Minjung theology cannot escape these questions because it chooses to locate Christ in history. As difficult as this path is, it is the only possibility for Christian ecumenism.

The ideology of conflict does not contribute positively to the enrichment of human life. It rather points the way to ever more sophisticated weapons. The concept of "enemy" is fixed in the scheme of conflict ideology. Minjung theology must, therefore, have "many stories" of suffering and hope to tell to the world. While it remains lively with "many stories" it will be able to keep itself from becoming an ideology. Many sincere stories will counteract self-righteousness wherever it may be found.

Culture

"Culture" is an ambiguous concept. There are "good" cultures and "bad" cultures. The former enhance, the latter impoverish. Culture is an ever-changing historical social reality. It is actively self-cultivating. Cultures, then, must be "evangelized." As Pope Paul VI proposes, "The split between the gospel and culture is without a doubt the drama of our time, just as it was of other times. Therefore every effort must be made to ensure a full evangelization of culture, or more correctly of cultures" (*Evangelii Nuntiandi*, 1975).

Is the suggestion made by Pope Paul VI practical in the cultural context of Korea today? Can the culture of Korea be evangelized? How is culture evangelized? Is it true that, being close to the frustration and aspiration of the people, minjung theology is uniquely equipped for this task? Is minjung theology perhaps too sensitive to the question of culture? Or do the minjung theologians see the distance between culture and the gospel as something that should be welcomed in order to make the message of the gospel clear to the world? Perhaps questions relating to "culture and gospel" are only posed by dominant members of society? What is the response of the minjung theologians to this papal suggestion?

Jeremiah says, "Woe to him who builds his house by unrighteousness." The subtle ways in which people build the house by unrighteousness differ from culture to culture as does the intensity or the lack of guilt that accompanies the building by unrighteousness and even the emotional overtones of words such as "woe" and "unrighteousness." The meanings of words such as hospitality and hostility, for instance, expand and shrink according to cultures. The world of cultures is one of perplexing varieties and differences. The reality of oppression itself is perceived differently from culture to culture. No culture is without some form of oppression. All cultures seem to find that a certain amount of oppression must be tolerated if the community as a whole is to function well.

Yet, all cultures are able to indicate some limiting tolerance level beyond which the oppression must be resisted. Intimations from culture, in its fundamental level, coincide with the intention of myth in that any given community should continue to exist. On the more conscious level, we observe that culture is dialectical in affirming and negating what its members cultivate. The effect is the imposition of some kind of control over chaos in the community. In short, culture is ambiguous, yet it tries to guard the community against chaos.

The cultural orientation of Korea is said to be predominantly Shamanistic. Kim Yong-bock indicates the Shamanistic background in the Korean word of "Hananim" for "God." He does this by quoting one paragraph from J. Robert Moore's *Village Life in Korea* (Nashville, Tennessee, 1911, p. 191). It is noteworthy that as much as we hear of the strong presence of the Shamanistic culture in Korea (a complex of religious rituals, spirituality, emotion, social life and sense of salvation associated with the activity and presence of the Shamans) we find only a few passing comments on Shamanism in *Minjung Theology: People as the Subjects of History*. Have the minjung theologians decided that the subject is not important? Are they suggesting that people should move radically from the Shamanistic connotations of God to a more precisely biblical image of God? Do they think that in achieving this quick transition discussions on Shamanism are not warranted? Are the theologians perhaps weary of the entanglement in discussions of syncretism which arise when they approach the subject of Shamanism seriously?

My humble and brief comments on this question are twofold.

1) The papal suggestion cannot be ignored if the minjung continue to be "the subjects of history" in minjung theology. The cultural life of the Korean people, as that of any people, must be a reality of enormous complexity. Now the questions that arise are: How do we evangelize culture? What is the value of such evangelization? How is such evangelization related to the elimination of social injustice and oppression?

2) Why is it that in *Minjung Theology: People as the Subjects of History*, so fascinating and creative, the use of the Bible is surprisingly meagre? Is it possible that the reason for this is that the minjung theologians are in general not interested in culture? Do they see in discussions of culture (or in culture-theology) only a maneuver on the part of the powerful, or of the intelligentsia to manipulate the poor? It seems to me that if theologians are interested in questions relating to culture, the Bible naturally will come into the discussion in a significant way.

How is it that both Hyun Young-hak and Suh Nam-dong (and other contributors to *Minjung Theology*) can narrate their theological interpretation of the people's cultural experience without bringing the words from the Bible to intersect the experience? I am not at all suggesting the desirability of a proof-text use of the Bible. But do the minjung theologians have a new approach to the use of the Bible in its relationship to understanding culture which the Christian *oikumeme* outside Korea has not yet shared?

I ask these questions because personally I find the Bible so extremely helpful in my understanding of human culture's relationship to divine revelation, and of the relationship between culture and social liberation. I take the position that the themes of "Christ and culture" and "Christ and liberation" are intimately related. It would seem that the living minjung theology must be engaged in the Korean language, the language of the culture of minjung. In a strict sense, a book on Korean minjung theology in English is a contradiction since English is not the language of the Korean minjung. The greatness of the Bible is that it can intertwine two dynamisms, revelation and culture, without destroying the contents of the revelation. In this intertwinement of revelation and culture we perceive: a) the reason why the study of culture is important; revelation does not come to us apart from culture; and b) culture's role (both positive and negative) in the process of liberation.

I conclude not with declarative remarks, but with questions.

Can minjung theology, while looking at the gospel with a Korean perspective, avoid including Korean understandings of humanity, nature, and ultimate reality as vital elements in the overarching content of the gospel?

How does the theology of "the sociopolitical biography of the Christian *koinonia* in Korea" incorporate this serious theological questioning about the relationship between culture and revelation? How does minjung theology incorporate the Korean culture into its message and practice of liberation?

However difficult it may be to respond to these, they are inevitable questions, and, I believe, crucial for the further growth of minjung theology.

LATIN AMERICAN
AND AFRICAN
RESPONSES

Story of Emille Bell
(From legend or possibly a true story)

I n Kyungju there is a famous Buddhist temple known
as Pulguksa which was built during the Silla Kingdom (57 B.C.E.-935 C.E.). Aside from the temple, what
strikes most visitors is the Emille Bell on the grounds of
the Kyungju National Museum. There, visitors hear the
story of the Emille Bell.

During the Silla Kingdom the devout Buddhist
Queen, Sunduk (Good Virtue), wanted to make a huge
bell as a sign of the people's dedication to Buddha. In
return, Buddha would then protect the nation from foreign invasions. The bell was to be placed in the national Buddhist temple in Kyungju.

The best bellmaker was appointed by the Queen to
build the best bell in the world. He did everything
right but failed to make the bell produce the finest
sound. He then consulted the religious leaders appointed by the Queen. They felt that a pure young maiden
should be melted into the bell in order to produce the
finest sound. By the order of the Queen, soldiers went
out to fetch a pure young maiden. On a poor farm village deep in the mountains they found a mother who
held a child. The soldiers took away the child, who
was crying, *"Emille, Emille* (Mother, Mother)."

The child was thrown into the melted iron that became the bell. Afterward the bell produced the sweet-
est and finest sound. The name of this bell came to be

known as the bell of Emille, because the beautiful sound ends with "*Emille, Emille, Emille* (Mother, Mother, Mother)." It is the sound of the child who calls her mother. The mother who hears it cries. The sound of Emille Bell, then, is the voice of *han*, the *han* of Korean women and children, that is, the *han* of the minjung.

A Latin American Looks
at Minjung Theology
by José Míguez Bonino

Introduction: Searching for an Approach

A couple of books and a few papers read, along with a visit to Korea of five days, may be more than enough to awaken a deep interest in and sympathy for minjung theology, but is hardly sufficient to justify writing a paper about it.

A Latin American who first discovers what is happening in churches and theology in Korea feels immediately attracted and moved by a sense of deep solidarity. Before engaging in analysis or conceptualization one seems to discern a fundamental commonality. Driven by this feeling one looks immediately for "analogies" and "correspondences" in the situation, in the nature and forms of the struggle and in theology. This is the first danger. It is easy to find a large number of such similarities. But are they real similarities or simply superficial coincidences? Do the same signs stand for the same realities in the two situations? Do similar words and expressions bear the same meaning or express the same intention?

The twofold danger of these extrapolations consists in projecting, into the reality of the other, one's concerns (thus simply "discovering" there what one has previously projected) and interpreting similarities which are really there from our own perspective (thus distorting the meaning that those realities have in their own context). Latin American theologians, who have experienced this "misunderstanding" on the part of some North Atlantic interpretations and who know how difficult it is to overcome such distortions, ought to be particularly careful not to do the same in relation to the struggle and reflection of our sisters and brothers from the Third World.

Should one then simply remain silent? Silence and admiration are the signs of respect. And a fraternal respect ought to be our first response. It lets the others "be," without trying to force them into our own concerns, categories or practices. On the other hand, respect does not exclude, but rather demands, an active reception of the word of the other. In this particular case it is difficult to suppress the deep impression of fundamental unity which persists, even if one discards the immediate similarities which suggest themselves at first sight.

We should resist, however, the temptation to arrive at premature syntheses or resolutions of our pluralities of experience, interpretation, and reflection. Nevertheless, we need to explore such pluralities in order to learn from them, to test our interpretations, to deepen and enrich our reflection.

It is in this spirit that I venture to reflect on what I have seen in minjung theology, in my admittedly limited and insufficient encounters. The structure of this paper is built around what I perceive as three main foci in minjung theology: minjung (the people), *han* and messianism.[1] I am trying in this way to avoid forcing the concerns of minjung theology into my own framework. I hope this can help in the kind of "active reception" which I think is necessary for fruitful dialogue.

Understanding Minjung in Context

"Minjung is a dangerous word," writes Suh Kwang-sun David. So, one might add, are the various words which in other languages would refer to the corresponding reality: people, *Volk*, *pueblo*, *popolo*. These are not equivalent words, despite what the dictionaries may say. Each one has its own connotation and history. And such differences are not purely linguistic; they represent different "social histories" of the realities that they denote. We cannot, therefore, presume to know what we are talking about when we say that "minjung" means people. This situation is somewhat paradoxical because those who "belong" in a given situation usually have no doubt identifying who belongs to "the people" and who doesn't. The reason for this paradox can be seen more clearly when we realize that we are not dealing simply with a sociological (theoretical) category but with a living reality which needs to be grasped also by means of "the social biography of the minjung."

When this word enters theology the complexity increases. To which biblical expressions can we refer? The self-evident terms *'am/ goyim* (Hebrew) or *laos* (Greek) are also "dangerous" words used in a variety of ways. But we soon find that certain connotations of minjung (and also *pueblo* in Spanish) would be better related to the Greek use of *ochlos* in the New Testament, or the reference to the *'apiru* in Hebrew history. Finally, words like *laos* have come in theology to function as ecclesiological terms, in such expressions as "the people of God" or even "laity."

Such complexity could mean confusion. But it can also mean richness that can be explored and appropriated. I try to single out some aspects which I seem to perceive in the Korean discussion and which we experience in our own way. It is clear that both in minjung and in Latin American liberation theology "people" does not stand simply for "human beings" (the generic use in English) nor for all the inhabitants or natives of a given country (population), nor for an ethnic entity (like *Volk* came to mean for German National Socialism). Hyun Young-hak speaks of "the ruled ones" (in opposition to the "rulers") and "the underdogs." Are we talking of a "social class"? Suh Nam-dong claims that "a study of the socioeconomic history of Korea is enabling us to grasp the reality of the minjung objectively." He also distinguishes the "peasant" and the "urban" minjung and comes close to a Marxist characterization when he distinguishes among the latter some who become activists and revolutionaries and adds, "the factory workers generally belong to this type." The Hegelian-Marxist distinction between a people (in Marxism a class) "in itself" and "for itself" belongs in the same universe of discourse.

Nobody, however, seems to be satisfied with an identification of minjung with "proletariat." Several reasons are given. Proletariat is a purely economic characterization, based on a "materialistic" philosophy ruled by determinism. Thus, proletariat is a "fixed category." The minjung, on the other hand, are a living organism, "a dynamic, changing concept" which transcends such fixed formulae. We could claim that this is a rather dry and wooden definition of proletariat, even on Marxist terms (although one meets it frequently in the Party catechisms).

But the issue is a deeper one. Our Latin American experience strongly corroborates the conviction that the classic Marxist definition of class and the corresponding tendency to reduce to epiphenomena everything else proves insufficient to analyze the social reality of "the people." On the one hand, can the concept of class, abstracted as a category of analysis from the historical situation of the working classes at the time of the industrial revolution in Europe, encompass the variety of experiences and situations of "the oppressed"?

Can cultural alienation, racial discrimination, and sexual oppression be simply understood as secondary effects of economic exploitation? Our answer is clearly: No! This is why we frequently prefer more embracing and richer terms like "the people," and "the poor" and usually identify them sociologically as the culturally oppressed, racially discriminated, and economically exploited majorities of our populations.

We face, however, a twofold question. What one gains in symbolic value in such comprehensive terms like "the people," "the poor," "the defeated of history" and so on, one loses in precision...and viceversa. We seem to need, on the one hand, to affirm the deep symbolic meaning of the richer terms and, on the other, to gain the analytical understanding of socioeconomic analysis. The identity of "the people" and their historical organic continuity cannot be explained simply in terms of the relations of economic production. But the *present historical situation* of this social reality of the people can hardly be understood aside from an understanding of the economic structures both at the transnational and national levels.

"The proletariat is defined socioeconomically, while the minjung is known politically," rightly asserts Kim Yong-bock. But can we really understand the political existence of the people in today's world bracketing out the social conditions, stratifications and determinations created by economic relations? The interesting distinction between the attitudes (and therefore the shaping of the consciousness) of different sectors within the minjung (rural, urban, factory workers) seems to answer this question. The rejection of economic reductionism, of monocausal explanations of reality, does not entail a refusal to recognize the importance of the economic factor, particularly in the world structures created by the universal expansion of the capitalist transnational network. The real task at this analytical level is to explore and clarify the relations and mutual determination of the different dimensions of the existence (and suffering) of "the people." In our situation, at least, we claim that *economic poverty* is not a sufficient but, alas, a necessary characterization of "the people." The study of the forms and relations of production (the economic system) seems therefore a necessary (though insufficient) form of knowing "the people."

Interpreting *Han*

The issue of the transcendence of the people, raised in the Korean discussion, seems to me to go further. It directs us away from the mere observation of a social entity to the perception of its subjectivity. This is what comes through forcefully to an interested observer in the central place given to *han*. To be sure, it is a category difficult to grasp analytically. The diversity of renderings proposed (some even mutually contradictory in appearance) warn us against superficial generalizations. "Righteous indignation," "a feeling of unresolved resentment," "repressed murmuring," "a tenacity of purpose" may seem a disparate collection of descriptions. But they make very clear and coherent sense when they are seen as a spectrum of responses of the collective subjectivity of the people as they are elicited at different moments, relations and circumstances. It may lead to resignation; it may find resolution through ritual (secular or religious), in dance, humor or story; it may erupt in rebellion; it may push for organized action. But such a variety of responses stems from a collective self-identity, a memory, an awareness which really "transcends" the material conditions of existence and which cannot be reduced to structural factors.

On the other hand, it is precisely this corporate identity that demands recognition and respect and refuses to be simply dissolved into a general category like "class" or even subsumed in a larger collective like "Third World" or "struggle for liberation." A theology which does not address this collective identity—or, better, a theology which is not conceived in the womb of this memory and experience—will always remain abstract and unrelated to the real life of the people, no matter how cleverly it may use sociological or economic tools to analyze the situation of the people, or how vigorously (and sincerely) it may claim to fight for their liberation.

We may, however, ask if such "collective identities" are culturally unique and therefore incommunicable. I think that both experience and reflection lead us to be more hopeful and positive, not only about the possibility of communication, but about significant exchange, mutual support and common reflection and initiative. In terms of experience, the work done now for a number of years under the auspices of the Ecumenical Association of Third World Theologians (EATWOT) with its international consultations, publications and exchanges, teaches us three things: 1) the irreducible singularity of a people's identity; 2) the deep solidarity, the "common language of experience" that is again and again discovered; and 3) (as we have already noted) the objective historical conditions which unite us all. (A number of similar experiences in other contexts could also be reported.) The pattern of an initial, mutual recognition, followed by the discovery of separate and distinct identities (not seldom including strong confrontation), and leading to a new awareness of unity in this diversity (which seems to be the movement in EATWOT) probably represents a necessary process.

The possibility of these experiences is, in my view, the result of two facts which we need to pursue in our future dialogue; one that has to do with this subjectivity of the people; the other with the future of the people. In the approximately 25 years of the gestation, birth and development of the theology of liberation in Latin America, we can speak of a first moment (on the part of sectors of the churches, particularly younger ministers and laymen) of awareness of the reality of the poor, the marginal, the exploited, and a sense of solidarity with them. The second moment (roughly from 1964 on) was marked by an intense concern for understanding the mechanisms of the creation and reproduction of these conditions, with a careful attention to socio-analytical tools. During the last ten years the growing experience in participation in the struggle of the people, the deeper encounter with their reality, the intense vitality of the growing base community movement, have led to a new understanding of what we have called the "spirituality" of the poor. Its particularity is given by the collective history of the peoples. Therefore it cannot be reduced to a common denominator.

The history of the populations with a long Native American tradition, of those who are almost exclusively the result of transplanting of European (mostly Mediterranean) immigrants and of the areas where the African presence (originating in slavery) has a decisive influence have generated peculiar traditions in religiosity, art, language, attitudes. The common factors for the vast majority of these peoples are the interrelated ones of the Spanish-Portuguese conquest and colonization and the religious conquest of evangelization. The story of our people is shaped in the matrix of the suffering of the oppression (military, economic, social, cultural) of the conquest and the comfort/alienation/hope of the Christian faith. The earlier memory (Native American, African) has been emptied into this matrix and can only be felt and recovered as it has been shaped by it (and, on the other hand, as it has itself informed it). For good or evil, then, the Latin American people are Christian—in the particular syncretisms which they have themselves created. This is their "spirituality," their subjective reality.

When we try to discover ways of describing or expressing the meaning of this spirituality, we use such terms as "solidarity," "persistence," "tenacity," a capacity to persist and resist in their own identity, for which we use sometime the Spanish word *terquedad* (literally "stubbornness"), "rebellion," protest but also resignation—curiously the same words that one finds in the translations of *han* or in the description of the black experience in the US. Moreover, such dimensions of the people's subjectivity find expression in their religious and cultural creations. I am not suggesting that this means that these traditions are interchangeable. But I am suggesting that the subjective responses of the people (here including the characterization as poor, oppressed, dominated) have a commonality, an inner structural (in the sense used in structuralist anthropology) unity which makes them communicable. This fact is important in two ways for a theology of and by the people. Ecumenically, because it makes possible an enriching exchange; hermeneutically, because it establishes a link with the biblical story in which God's presence and action is manifested in good measure in suffering and response, the spirituality of the people (the *'apiru*, the *am-ha'aretz*, the *ochlos*).

The other side of the question, intimately related with the first, has to do with the future of the people. They are "subjects of history," not in the same sense as those who hold power but in the sense that their reality persists through history, keeps its continuity through crises and upheavals, retains a "memory" and thus "transcends" history. But are they also to become the inheritors of power? Is there a "messianic" promise for the "people"? If so, is there an active role for them in the fulfillment of this promise?

The dialectics of the problem are clearly brought out by Moon Hee-suk Cyris (however one might evaluate his hermeneutics, particularly in relating Genesis and the prophetic writings). On the one hand, the minjung are, as in Micah, "the have-nots, the oppressed and the alienated." But, over against this sociological characterization, theology must see them as the humanity created to take charge of creation. Exodus, then, has to be read as a restoration of this original right. In that sense, they are the object of God's liberation. Moon, then, rightly asks "whether YHWH was the sole actor in the movement for their liberation." And he answers: "God asks the human, who is created in God's image, to act as...partner. *People are to assist in the restoration of their rights*" (emphasis mine). Since the oppressed are "concerned mainly about surviving" and therefore unwilling to struggle for their liberation, there is a prophetic task of calling back the people to their original right to be masters of creation, not of other people, and thus join in the struggle for their liberation. In the history of the minjung this active role has been present, and, as several minjung theologians indicate, it is possible to trace this history of liberation. Moreover, some claim that the Christian faith has been assimilated by the Korean people within this tradition of political resistance to oppression.

Messianism and Socioeconomic Structures

But what is the relation between this messianism in the minjung tradition and the power struggle that determines the objective socioeconomic structures of our world? Kim Yong-bock pursues this question contrasting "messianic" politics and the "political messianism" of the different systems competing for power in recent Korean history: Japanese nationalistic imperialism, Marxist communism and Western technocracy. The messianic politics in which the minjung develop their subjective identity, transcending the determinisms of history, does not rest in the alienating power of "political messianisms." It is always an "already" and a "not yet." In building their own memories, their stories, they become real subjects of history, "refusing to be condemned to the fate of being objects of manipulation and suppression." In dance, for instance, the feeling of *han* is resolved. Even when the religious dimension is not specifically present, there is a sense of transcendence. But it is in the Christian story where we find the Suffering Messiah which fulfills "the two messianic qualities of identification with the suffering people and functioning as servant to the aspirations of the people for liberation."

The strong emphasis that Kim places on subjectivity/subjecthood, on transcending history symbolically (story, dance, memory), and on the suffering of the people seems to suggest that he is not deeply concerned about political transformation. In fact, he strongly contrasts the power of the minjung with "the politics of power." This does not seem to correspond entirely to Kim's intention. In fact, he speaks of "a Christian political perspective which includes concrete structural elements: "*Shalom* in relation to the unification of Korea [and] *koinonia* (participation) and justice in relation to the social and political development of Korean history...." This requires one "to tackle the issue of power in a political struggle." Here, he seems to hesitate: There is for him an ultimate incompatibility between "power as we now know it" and the Messianic Kingdom, the powerless status of Jesus the Messiah and the people." Nevertheless, in pursuing the goals indicated above, it seems that "some tamed measure of political realism should be allowed...."

Critical Concerns

I find here one of the most critical questions in our theological conversation. I would like to raise it in two different perspectives. The first one has to do with our present historical experience of the people's plight in "Western technocracy" (or, for that matter, in the "communism" that Kim describes).

Can we really say that the uprooted and marginalized masses thrown into the ghettoes of the monstrous cities of the Third World keep the memory, the continuity of the subjecthood, even the symbolical transcendence of history? Are we taking seriously the effects of this brutal de-personalizing (the non-person), de-socializing, massification of people? In Latin America this is a burning issue and a much debated problem.

Some claim that this folk religiosity (our form of *han*) contains the potential for transformation; others believe that it will be radically dissolved by modernity. But all are convinced that a new awareness, a conscious commitment to the transformation symbolically represented in the subjective consciousness of the people, is absolutely necessary. In fact, the only alternative to a totalitarian socialism or a technocratic de-humanization is the birth of a consciousness which keeps a continuity with the memory of the people but has gained a new awareness and lucidity. In our situation the basic ecclesial communities are, to a large extent, the matrix of this re-born nucleus of the people. This is why we frequently give a threefold definition of "the people": 1) the poor and oppressed, the marginalized; 2) those among them who become aware of themselves and their condition and assume the cause of their liberation; and 3) those who opt for the poor and place themselves in solidarity with them in their historical struggle. This definition should not be understood as three distinct groups or even as a sort of ladder, but as the description of a process of growth within the single reality of the people, as the development of "the subjectivity/ subjecthood" of the people, to use Kim Yong-bock's term.

Kim Yong-bock is evidently concerned to emphasize the discontinuity between "messianic politics" and "power, as we know it." If such discontinuity would be absolutized, we would end up in pure subjectivity. Kim, however, tries to maintain a more dialectical relation: there has been and there is a "continuous contradiction" between dominating power and "the power of the people" as the history of minjung resistance proves. In this contradiction, there is no hesitation about the place where the minjung (and minjung theology) will stand. It is here that he admits, somewhat reluctantly, "some tame measure of political realism." Is this kind of unwilling concession ("allowed" is the term he uses) an adequate articulation for the active role of the people in history? It seems to me that Kim moves beyond it in two ways.

On the one hand, by rejecting "an absolute political cynicism or 'realpolitik'" and on the other hand, by asking that "the notion of people's power...be taken into account." If these two observations are put together we have, I think: 1) the recognition of "people's power" as legitimate historical embodiment of minjung subjecthood in the arena of political struggle, and 2) the need of a political ethics congruent with the nature of the people's concerns (*justice*, *koinonia* and *shalom*) and aware of the relative autonomy of the realm of political life ("political realism"). It is, I think, in this direction that we should pursue the dialogue.

Why is Kim so concerned with emphasizing discontinuity? Quite clearly, because of the persistence of elements of political messianism (at one point he speaks of "self-righteousness and triumphalism") which have come from the ideology of Christendom. I think this is absolutely right and I and other Latin American liberation theologians would agree totally with his affirmation that "it may be one of the critical tasks, especially of Third World theologians, to purge elements of political messianism from our Christian confessions, proclamations and theologies." Can we do this and still establish between our faith and our political struggle a more significant and intrinsic relation than a last moment concession? I would like to suggest two areas of reflection in this direction.

One has to do with the mediations of our faith. Faith is, no doubt, an absolute relation to the transcendent. But such relation exists only concretely, particularly in psychological and social conditions: attitudes, ethical decisions, ideological perspectives, social positions. These objective and subjective conditions in time and space have their own autonomous laws and characteristics. The operation of political power as we know it is no less autonomous—but also no more—than the realm of culture, of subjectivity, even of the religious institutions and manifestations which are quite rightly vindicated as an irreducible dimension of the life of "the people." These are no less mediations than political relations of power, class or race. If this is so, I see no reason to mistrust them more than we do the rest. To see them as constitutive categories of our theological reflection seems to me as necessary as to see the cultural identity in the same fashion. The "transcendent" subjecthood of the people can only be assumed, critically assessed and historically realized in concrete, historical projects. This is what we are trying to do in the Latin American theology of liberation.

Finally, I would raise a question which is equally addressed to Korean and Latin American theology. It has to do with the identification of Jesus Christ with "the people" or "the poor." To say that Jesus identified himself with the people or the poor is one thing. To say that the latter are "identical" with Jesus Christ is a different proposition. When it is done—and I think we frequently come quite close to it—I wonder whether we are not implicitly assuming some form of "messianic" confusion, whether it is political, cultural, ethnic or otherwise.

In this sense an expression such as "to evolve in a concrete way a *Christian* political perspective" or that "the relationship between the minjung and the messiah should be understood as the relation between the minjung as the subject and the messiah as their function" seems to me on the outside limits of a healthy identification. If misunderstood it can dissolve the concrete historicity of Jesus the Christ and thus also its significance as the symbol of the dialectics transcendence/incarnation which seems to me essential both for the identity of the Christian faith and for the "openness" of the project of the people.

It is in this sense that the notion of mediation seems to us to keep this dialectics open and fruitful. I fully realize that there are in the Korean religious and social history dimensions which are different from our situation and which require a reflection which we have not so far clarified for ourselves. It is for this reason that I formulate these comments very tentatively, more as an attempt to recognize, appreciate and let us be challenged by minjung theology than as a critique or an evaluation. If my comments can foster dialogue, they will have served this purpose.

Note

1. I have taken these headings from Suh Kwang-sun David's introductory paper in *Minjung Theology: People as the Subjects of History* (Maryknoll, London, Singapore: Orbis, Zed, CCA, 1983). This excellent collection of essays has been my best introduction to minjung theology. Quotations in the text refer to this volume.

Heaven

(From *The Dawn of Labor* by Park No-hae, Seoul, 1984, translated by Jung Young Lee)

My employer who gives food for my family
Is my heaven.

When I go to the hospital
With hands pressed by a machine,
The doctor who can give
And take away my life
Is my heaven.

Without wages for two months
I was taken by police, for
I organized a Labor Union.
The policeman who takes an innocent person
Is my horrible heaven.

The judge who can make me guilty or innocent
Is my fearful heaven.

The officer who sits in the office and
Can help or destroy me
Is my fearful heaven.

The person of high position,
The powerful person, and
The Rich person
Are all heavenly beings.

And What of Culture?:
An African Reflection
on Minjung Theology
by Kwesi A. Dickson

Introduction

The main thesis of minjung theology, based on my reading of the book *Minjung Theology: People as the Subjects of History*, is all too familiar and crucial: the church in Korea must take a fresh look at its theology. But this must happen not with a view to manipulating the received Western theology so that it appears relevant to its new locus. The objective of the new critical approach must be to establish new ground rules for theologizing—a theologizing that has in mind the particularity of the Korean situation. Hence the essays in *Minjung Theology* represent both a rejection and an affirmation: Western theology does not speak to the Korean situation and is therefore largely irrelevant. What is needed is the kind of theology which has Korean culture and history as its context.

This conviction, which has been articulated in various ways by a growing body of theologians, undergirds much of the theological discussions and developments which have taken place in the Third World in the last few decades. I have read *Minjung Theology* as an African who has followed these discussions and developments and consequently did not have any difficulty sharing the basic concerns behind them. It is of particular interest to me that unlike other expressions of liberation theology,[1] minjung theology affirms Korean culture and history as indispensable to theologizing. In some theological circles this cultural emphasis has been seen as involving a disengagement from the harsh realities of contemporary life. This kind of assessment arises from a view of culture as a fossil which excites interest only by its quaintness, but which, by its very "outdatedness," represents an escape from the "real" world. These Korean theologians speak from a firsthand experience of a *living* culture which gives a distinctive shape to the life of the Korean people. A culture which gives shape to the life of a people, including Christians, cannot be ignored.

Culture and History: Differing Legacies

This insistence upon the importance of culture and history is one with which many in Africa can identify, for by and large African theologians insist on giving culture a key role in theologizing. Of course, Africa south of the Sahara has produced a variety of theological voices: black theology from South Africa has, generally speaking, given little or no attention to culture, while in the rest of sub-Saharan Africa two main approaches to culture as a theological factor have surfaced. According to some, culture plays the role of giving Western theology an adaptive dimension, a procedure often described as indigenization, while according to others, culture is to play the much more fundamental role of providing a base from which to gain a fresh understanding of faith in Christ.

With respect to these two culture-based approaches, it is important to note that the protagonists of minjung theology express their disillusionment with such issues as indigenization,[2] for minjung theologians argue that theological exercise which proceeds on the basis of indigenization assumes the normative character of the received Western theology, and only serves to endorse the erroneous belief that theology is done in some cultural contexts, and not in others. I hold the conviction that the latter of the two culture-based approaches is the only sound way of thinking through the Christian deposit and gaining fresh and relevant insight into the Christian faith.

The issue, then, is not the advisability of giving recognition to our cultural particularities: *How* culture is to inform theologizing is the real issue, and this is where I find *Minjung Theology* both helpful and puzzling.

I must confess at this juncture that I am operating under a severe disability: my knowledge of the Korean situation is very limited—it does not go much beyond what is revealed in these essays, hence my reluctance to make a detailed assessment of these essays in terms of the extent to which they do justice to the Korean situation. I am also unable to fully explore how far comparisons may be made between the analyses done in these essays and the culture-based approach adopted by a number of African theologians. Nevertheless, I discern in these essays a number of ideas which I would like to comment on given my own background.

To begin with, although the colonial history of Korea shares some characteristics with colonialism in Africa, there are important differences. The colonization of Africa was done by peoples from the West, that is, by peoples of a distinctly different culture. Furthermore, colonial expansion in Africa was often done in association with missionary expansion, so that, in the minds of many, African missions are not easily separated from colonial rule. Today almost all African countries are independent. Independence, however, has not meant the obliteration of the colonial influence which is present in the educational system, in church life and thought, and in the continued use of the colonizers' languages as the official medium of communication. There are in Africa, of course, variations on this theme—Africa is not uniform. In eastern Africa, for example, Swahili has united millions of Africans as they express themselves in a language they are able to use with consummate facility. But even in this part of Africa the colonial influence is still present in many ways. The cultural impact of this colonial influence does not need to be spelled out; independence has not made too much difference, generally speaking. Indeed, it is not entirely accidental, perhaps, that many an African government encourages the kind of rule characterized by master-servant relations; this is particularly true of military dictatorships which have become such a glaring part of the African political scene.

Korea's political history has been different in some important respects. Not only has it been ruled throughout its history by *indigenous* aristocracies and autocracies, with the exception of the Japanese imperialist period beginning with the annexation of Korea in 1910, but also Korea has not had to adopt a foreign language and thereby incur serious damage to its cultural life. Thus it can be said—and I believe this is not a totally inaccurate comment—that in the last four centuries or so African culture has been under greater stress than Korean culture. Judging by the references to Korean life in these essays it is clear that "Koreanness" has not entirely given way in Korea's struggle against indigenous autocracies and imperialism; indeed there is some indication in some of the essays of an interest in the cultural practices from the past.

Having said that, let me also observe that, the avowals of commitment to Korean culture notwithstanding, the minjung theology to which I have been exposed does not tell us nearly enough about Korean culture. As a matter of fact, Hyun Young-hak's "A Theological Look at the Mask Dance in Korea" in *Minjung Theology* is one of the few examples which gives readers some insight into Korea's cultural life. Yet despite the stated commitment to culture, one is given little real insight into what the authors' understanding of culture as a theological factor is. The analysis that follows explicates my assessment.

The Minjung Treatment of Culture

To begin with, one minjung theologian, Suh Kwang-sun David, states: "...the social history of the minjung liberation and messianic movements, the minjung religious traditions (both Buddhist and Donghak), and the past and the present cultural expressions of the minjung are all being studied as one of the two important reference points for minjung theology" (*Minjung Theology*, p. 42). This statement, clear as it is, does not resolve the issue of culture's role beyond highlighting the minjung—the poor and the oppressed majority—whose liberation should be the church's goal, as other statements make abundantly clear. Hyun Young-hak's work on the Mask Dance (*Minjung Theology*, Chapter 3) is relevant here. In this dance, according to the author, the minjung "experience and express a critical transcendence over this world and laugh at its absurdity. By satirizing the aristocrats they stand over against the aristocrats (*Minjung Theology*, p. 50). In performing these dances, "catharsis may happen, but there would be no changes in the concrete everyday life. The minjung thus become fatalistic" (*Minjung Theology*, p. 52). Nevertheless, these dances "create in the minjung the wisdom and the power to survive," and "the experience provides the minjung with the courage to fight for change and freedom" (*Ibid.*).

These references suggest to me that the Mask Dance is seen in a limited way: this cultural expression enables the minjung to experience self-transcendence and to resist oppression. But the question that arises for me, and to which no sufficiently clear answer is available as far as these essays are concerned, is: *Do these and other cultural expressions provide insights to aid theological speculation and formulation, in such a way that the minjung would recognize themselves in that theology?* In this connection, Suh Kwang-sun David makes a candid statement: "While dissociating ourselves from imported models, we cannot in fact claim that minjung theology is *the* Korean theology, if by Korean theology we mean what is acceptable to the majority of Korean churchgoers and theologians. Although it is rapidly making inroads into the Christian community, beginning with the marginal elements, it is still a Korean theology in the making. It is *a* Korean theology for the future and of the future which is emerging out of the reflections and experiences of the Korean reality at this particular time in history" (*Minjung Theology*, p. 17).

The admission made here is important. That is, that minjung theology is yet to become that with which Korean Christians can readily identify. Suh Kwang-sun David does not give us any indication of the process by which minjung theology would have to develop so as to become acceptable to the minjung. Is it going to have to be more culturally integrated? There is quite a difference between recognizing a cultural reality, and making that reality a vehicle for theological expression. Whether the latter mode of development is what is anticipated or not, I am not in a position to say, but I would have thought that the concern for the minjung displayed by minjung theologians would call for a culture that provides a vehicle for the expression of faith in Christ. To express Christian thought in such a way that it speaks to a people's apprehension of Christ against the background of its life and thought would seem to me to be an unavoidable task. With respect to this, the words of Suh Nam-dong on the need to move away from the theological status quo are worth quoting: "Let us hold in abeyance discussions on doctrines and theories about sin which are heavily charged with the bias of the ruling class and are often nothing more than the labels the ruling class uses for the deprived. Instead, we should take *han* as our theme, which is indeed the language of the minjung and signifies the reality of their experience" (*Minjung Theology*, p. 68).

The statement quoted above not only indicates the Korean theologians' desire not to bend to inherited theological models, but also highlights what is undoubtedly the preoccupation of the theologians—justice for the poor, a theme which is sounded in all the essays. This concern for the underprivileged is stated very succinctly by Hyun Young-hak when he writes that God in Christ "has a special concern for the underdogs, namely, the minjung. Otherwise, the Christian God would have no place in our history, in the events of our time, or for that matter in the future" (*Minjung Theology*, p. 53). References of this kind abound in these essays, leaving us no room for doubt about the real concern of their authors: to express Christ's love for the poor as against the oppressors.

The Poor and Powerful: A Matter of Emphasis or Favoritism

It is perhaps an understatement that a sharp distinction is drawn between the powerful and the poor in minjung theology, with the latter being held as the ones in whom God shows interest. Let me once again confess my ignorance of the Korean situation; I can only approach the ideas being expressed by the Korean theologians having in mind my African experience. It is undeniable that many in Africa have been victims of the harsh hand of poverty and oppression. Military and civilian dictatorships have caused such havoc in Africa, and the sad fact about dictatorships is that since their creators cannot see any alternatives to themselves they strive, through even harsher methods, to stay in power. (Incidentally, modern dictatorships are in contrast to traditional rule whereby, no matter how powerful a chief or ruling elders might be, there are tried and unavoidable ways and means of removing, or at least controlling, dictatorial tendencies. It is of interest to know, for example, that among the Asante of Ghana the chief first swears allegiance to his people, *before* the people swear allegiance to him, a clear indication of how the chief's role is understood. In other words, chiefs are not free to lord power over their subjects. Sadly, this understanding of government has not influenced the rulers of many African states, even allowing for the fact that in some respects the poor may have contributed to their own impoverishment, as Hyun Young-hak observes with respect to the Korean situation [*Minjung Theology*, p. 138 f.]).

What is distinctive about my encounter with minjung theology is not its witness to the presence of the poor and the oppressed; it is the theology woven around this commitment that occasions some surprise. I do believe with these theologians that God has a special concern for the underdogs, but I have problems believing that this implies the corollary of God writing off the proud and the powerful. It is worthwhile recalling some of the more significant convictions expressed about the poor. Thus we are told that the minjung are the "sinners, the tax collectors, the sick, those who opposed the powers in Jerusalem, the despised people of Galilee, the prostitutes, etc." The types of people mentioned here were those whom Jesus addressed. Indeed, Jesus "was the personification of the minjung and their symbol" (*Minjung Theology*, p. 159), and "It is our conviction," Suh Nam-dong writes, "that the Risen Jesus lives among the minjung, who have been continually oppressed and alienated in the course of socioeconomic history" (*Minjung Theology*, p.161). It is for the minjung that Jesus died, and he "rose from the dead so that the minjung may rise from the power of death historically and not just at the end of time" (*Minjung Theology*, p. 187).

These statements come from Christians who evidently feel strongly about the socioeconomic and political conditions in Korea; they represent a deep sense of commitment to the poor and the disadvantaged. The clear impression one gains from these and other passages in the essays making up *Minjung Theology* is that the majority of the people are held in thrall by the small ruling class. Of course, the minjung are not entirely white-washed, as already observed. Hyun Young-hak speaks of minjung who are "subservient, conservative and reactionary," "the ones whom those who work for the minjung consider a 'headache'"; others are opportunistic and serve the rulers (*Minjung Theology*, p. 52). Nevertheless, the conviction is firmly expressed: everything must be done to break the hold of the powerful over the powerless, and this conviction comes from reflecting upon the Scriptures, as the essays by Moon Hee-suk Cyris, Ahn Byung-mu and Suh Nam-dong, in particular, show (*Minjung Theology*, Chapters 7, 8 and 9 respectively).

Now from the point of view of cultural emphasis, which some of us favor, there are two main, and concomitant, aspects of the Christian's approach to the issue of oppression and impoverishment of one group by another. These are the biblical evidence of concern and love for the poor and a study of traditional ideas and practices for evidence of traditional attitudes toward misrule. This latter aspect is very important, for Christian strategy against misrule should be influenced by it.

Let us take these two aspects one after the other, having in mind the book under consideration.

That the Scriptures do witness to God's concern for the poor goes without question, and it would be pointless to attempt an assembling, no matter how limited, of the biblical evidence; some of this evidence is already before us in these essays. One gets the impression, however, that sometimes the scriptural texts are interpreted in a somewhat tendentious way. One example of such an interpretation will suffice. Commenting on Jesus' assertion, "I came not to call the righteous, but sinners" (Mk 2:17b), Ahn Byung-mu writes: "Jesus never showed what may be called universal love. He loved people with partiality. He always stood on the side of the oppressed, the aggrieved, and the weak" (*Minjung Theology*, p. 146). That Jesus took the side of the weak goes without saying; after all, Jesus' Jewish background taught that God's justice involved his taking the side of the poor and the oppressed. Ahn Byung-mu, however, seems simply to equate "the righteous" in this biblical passage with the rich and the powerful. It is my conviction that this equation only does partial justice to the significance of *dikaioi* in that passage. By this word Jesus is referring to those who considered themselves to have no need for Jesus' message of salvation, those who, believing that they were healthy, considered the services of a doctor irrelevant. Among such could be both rich and poor. Similarly, "sinners" in this context can only mean those who acknowledge their spiritual insufficiency and are ready to rely upon God. If by "[Jesus] loved people with partiality" Ahn Byung-mu is saying that Jesus could not love the rich also, under any circumstances, he would be making an assertion which I would have problems accepting, and indeed the biblical evidence is not so one-sided.

It is in line with Ahn Byung-mu's analysis that Suh Nam-dong speaks of the risen Jesus living among the minjung. This, in my judgment, is to restrict Jesus' love and power unacceptably. Jesus' death and resurrection are a judgment on our *human pride* which presumes to put our will above God's.

The "Cultural Particularity" of Biblical Exegesis
Now it is doubtful whether the New Testament evidence allows one to restrict God's love in the ways illustrated in the statements above. Thus Jesus did criticize "the laws of Judaism, especially the Sabbath law...." He also "publicly challenged the regulations imposed by the priestly rulers of the Jerusalem Temple, which was the central organization exploiting the minjung" (*Minjung Theology*, p. 161). Nevertheless, Jesus did not cut himself off from Judaism; he decried its excesses without wanting it thrown on to the dust heap of forgotten things. Jesus was desirous of rescuing the

rich from their conceit; that the rich young ruler went away sad because Jesus had asked him to sell his property and distribute it to the poor is indication of Jesus' concern for those who had allowed wealth and power to blind them to the greater wealth of the kingdom (Luke 18:18f). On the cross Jesus pronounced forgiveness upon the powers who were determined to end his life (Luke 23:34). The Book of the Acts of the Apostles is a witness to the possibility of the influential in society being brought to the knowledge of salvation. Thus Cornelius, a centurion, was baptized by Peter (Acts 10:1 ff), and in the course of Paul's preaching many "believed, with not a few Greek women of high standing as well as men" (Acts 17:12). Indeed, the very dedication of the Gospel of Luke and of Acts may be seen as an acknowledgment of the power of the gospel in the lives of the rich and powerful.

The above comments have been made for the purpose, at least in part, of expressing a point of considerable importance with respect to the Scriptures, a point which, speaking from my cultural perspective, is one which has a very important bearing upon theologizing out of one's cultural situation: The Bible has a cultural particularity which must be recognized, or one runs the risk of assuming that the Bible has answers to all the issues we are raising today in our respective national circumstances. To say this as an African is not to sound contradictory, for even though it is a fact that there is much in common—in ideas, customs, expressions, etc.—between the world of the Bible and African life and thought, it is undeniable that the existential questions being raised in Africa today were not before those who wrote/compiled the books of the Bible.

In effect, I am asking whether or not the minjung analysis done of certain biblical passages shows full cognizance of this cultural particularity of the Scriptures. It is with much hesitation that I bring up this issue, given the limited extent of my knowledge of Korea or minjung theology, but it is an issue which deserves serious consideration if we are to do justice to the Scriptures and also to the situations themselves which are connected to biblical exegesis.

Before we take a brief look at the issues of whether or not cultural ideas and practices give sanction for dictatorial rule, let us turn to the keyword "minjung" and what it means. The words of Suh Kwang-sun David are instructive in this connection: "The minjung is present where there is sociocultural alienation, economic exploitation, and political suppression. Therefore, a woman is a minjung when she is dominated by man, by the family, or by socio-cultural structures and factors. An ethnic group is a minjung group when it is politically and economically discriminated against by another ethnic group. A race is minjung when it is dominated by another ruling race. When intellectuals are suppressed for using their creative and critical abilities against rulers on behalf of the oppressed, then they too belong to the minjung. Workers and farmers are minjung when they are exploited, their needs and demands are ignored, and they are crushed down by the ruling powers" (*Minjung Theology*, pp. 35-36).

If I were to be invited to say, having Africa in mind, whether or not the categories of minjung referred to above could be expanded, I would identify, without the slightest hesitation, the powerful, the rulers, the oppressors. Many an African government is as oppressed as the people over whom unwholesome rule is exercised. To explicate this statement one could mention the borrowing of the ideologies developed in other cultural contexts; the preoccupation with internal security, which involves the acquisition of arms at great cost, for the suppression of political opponents; the inability, or lack of will, to solve economic and other problems; the constant blaming of all internal problems on external sources, etc. Indeed, in a very real sense, many an African ruler is a minjung, because he or she is oppressed by the very system which has been devised for the oppression of others. In many ways they are less free than those whose freedom they seek to take away.

Including Oppressors: A Challenge to Minjung Theology?
Would this way of looking at oppression and its perpetrators be acceptable to minjung theologians? I cannot say, and I certainly do not wish to appear to be suggesting that these Korean theologians' understanding of Korea's socioeconomic and political situation is not authentic. It would be very presumptuous of me to suggest this, given my lack of knowledge of Korean conditions. In all these comments I have endeavored to keep in mind the question of how these theological discussions can be viewed in the light of the African cultural situation.

There is an interesting biblical passage, Isaiah 14, which raises the issue of the goal of the struggle for freedom: Is it the enslavement of the oppressor? Or is it the oppressor's rehabilitation? The Isaiah passage gloats over the downfall of the Babylonian oppressors; more than that, the people of Israel "will take captive those who were their captors, and rule over those who oppressed them." Now no one would argue, surely, that there is virtue in being an oppressor; after all the concept of justice cannot be separated from that of love. In African society wrong-doing is not only frowned upon, but also condemned; indeed wrong-doers may even be expelled. Nevertheless, the main goal of society is to have its stability strengthened, and rulers know that dictatorial rule will not be tolerated indefinitely. Furthermore, there are avenues for the rehabilitation of those who are found working against society's interests.

As a final comment on minjung theology, I am unable to make any meaningful comment on whether or not Korean culture encourages dictatorial rule, though possibly the coups and rebellions about which Choo Chai-yong writes may have been influenced by a cultural necessity (*Minjung Theology*, Chapter 5). Where the traditional cultural reality is not in favor of oppressive rule and the impoverishment of the ruled, then of course the biblical teaching finds a ready ally. Where the cultural situation, however, does not frown upon arbitrary rule, then the task of influencing ideas in favor of freedom and partnership becomes more difficult.

I do not have a ready solution with respect to the latter. My interest in bringing it up is to reiterate the point already made, that knowing in precise terms what traditional thinking is, is essential to the Christian task of relating to the world.

Notes

1. I am using this expression loosely to characterize, in particular, Latin American liberation theology, black theology (from both North America and South Africa) and political theology.

2. See Suh Kwang-sun David's essay, "Korean Theological Development in the 1970s," *Minjung Theology: People as the Subjects of History* (Maryknoll, London, Singapore: Orbis, Zed, CCA, 1983), pp. 38-43. Because of the frequency with which I refer to this volume, all further references to *Minjung Theology* will be included in the text.

APPENDICES

A Letter to the Minjung Theologians of Korea

by Herwig Wagner

Professor Dr. Herwig Wagner is chairperson of the Theological Commission of the Evangelisches Missionswerk, *the Protestant Association for World Mission, based in Hamburg, West Germany. His article was written in conjunction with the other members of the Theological Commission: Dr. Theo Ahrens, Dr. Winfried Glüer, Dr. Klaus Gruhn, Dr. Wolfgang Günther, Dr. Siegfried Liebschner, Dr. Christine Lienemann-Perrin, Dr. Paul Löffler, Frau Annette Nuber, Prof. Dr. Lother Schreiner, Dr. Ludwig Wiedenmann, S.J., and Dr. Joachim Wietzke.*

The theological committee of the *Evangelisches Missionswerk* is an interconfessional group of twelve members from missionary organizations and teaching and research institutions and from among the parish priests of the German Federal Republic and West Berlin; for approximately two years this group has studied minjung theology. We have chosen this theology as a paradigm within the framework of our overall theme, "Methods and Form of Present-day Missionary Activity," because we see minjung theology as an independent theological approach that reflects a specific context but at the same time has ecumenical relevance.

We have discussed the published material available to us in German and English, paying special attention to *Minjung Theology: People as the Subjects of History*, edited by the Commission on Theological Concerns of the Christian Conference of Asia (Maryknoll, London, Singapore: Orbis, Zed, CCA, 1983). (Otherwise unidentified quotations in our letter are from this book.)

Our intention in the following remarks and queries is to initiate a direct ecumenical dialogue with you, the minjung theologians of Korea. We are deeply moved by what we know of the life and suffering of Christian communities within the Korean minjung, and we are impressed by your efforts to reflect theologically on these experiences and to do so in concrete solidarity.

We enter into the dialogue with openness and a willingness to learn. At the same time, we think that in ecumenical dialogue we owe it to each other to ask crucial questions. We urge you, therefore, not to view our questions as a form of theological superciliousness but as an honest quest for better understanding. The ecumenical learning process depends on dialogue, and we will therefore be grateful if you in turn are frank in expressing your criticism of our remarks or of the theological positions now prevalent in the German Federal Republic.

In the first part of our letter we look, by way of an example, into a question that has occupied us in our discussions: the relation between eschatology and the building of the world. In the second part we voice questions that arise in our minds with regard to other aspects of minjung theology; we have discussed these as well, but in this letter we can only mention them briefly. We regard them as important, however, for further study and dialogue with you. In the third and final part of the letter we try to formulate some questions with regard to our own theological thinking and activity.

We are aware that minjung theology is not, and is not meant to be, a unified system after the manner of a theological dogmatics. We know, too, that minjung theologians adopt divergent positions. But since we cannot take part in the discussion going on in Korea, we must necessarily generalize and speak simply of "minjung theology." This is another reason why we need your critical response to our letter.

Hope of God's Reign and Sociopolitical Objectives
In the Western churches, and in missionary activity originating in the West, concern for the salvation of the individual and for the gathering of a community has usually been so much to the fore that God's universal claim to all areas of life has received little attention. In order to avoid this narrow focus, minjung theology develops the biblical understanding of "the kingdom of God" by relating it concretely to the history and social reality of the Korean

people. It locates the missionary task of the church in a radically eschatological context, refusing to water it down by "existential interpretation" or reduction to a "social gospel."

We regard your exegetical studies (especially those of Ahn Byung-mu) as examples of the sociohistorical interpretation of the Bible to which increasing attention is also being given in Western theology (for example, Theissen, Schottroff, Crüsemann, and Gottwald, to speak only of Germany).

This approach is then consistently developed in systematic, socioethical writings. Thus Kim Yong-bock, for example, argues the thesis of a resurrection of the minjung within history; he takes minjung here to be a relational concept, not a set of social classes. Christ is with those who are "below," and "messianic politics," in contrast to "political messianism," correspondingly rejects every form of the exercise of political rule and power.

The writings of Suh Nam-dong and Choo Chai-yong on general history and church history illustrate the kind of intra-historical dynamisms that have been triggered by uncompromising "political visions." Even though the "messianic" hopes of the minjung have been repeatedly frustrated because of the intervention of the powerful, these same hopes have nonetheless been a decisive factor in the process whereby "the people have become active subjects" in the history of Korea. With these experiences as your background, you think it cynical to expect those who suffer to submit to their destiny and hope for a better life in the next world. Suh Nam-dong therefore justifiably pleads for the revival of "paradigms from the history of the Church" (161), such as "the millennium," which embrace not only the salvation of the individual but also the renewal of "the whole social reality" that God has promised.

The eschatological refusal of compromise that characterizes minjung theology serves as a salutary and necessary criticism of the European ecclesial tradition which has wrongly involved itself in many mistaken compromises and conformities. On the one hand, then, we can agree with you; on the other, the expectation of an intra-historical kingdom of God, such as characterizes the minjung communities and minjung theology, troubles us. We can perhaps clarify our reservations by citing the example of the uncompromising and comprehensive criticism of power in minjung theology, a criticism that aims at bringing about a state of things in which no domination of any kind is exercised.

In your expositions of this theme you describe the realization of the kingdom as a process that is moving toward an intra-historical goal, namely, the state in which the minjung are fully "active subjects." In the phase before this final state, "the minjung suffer under their historical predicament," as Kim Yong-bock puts it. The minjung are in conflict with their opponent, embodied in the possessors of political, economic, and cultural power, who block the attainment by the minjung of their full status as active subject. When the question is raised of how the minjung are to carry on their struggle with the possessors of power, who if need be resort to oppression, exploitation, and deprivation of freedom, the minjung answer with a call for an unlimited renunciation of power, domination, and force. The "messianic" minjung (it is said) are not only powerless (*ohnmächtig*) when they are oppressed, but they continue to be "power-less" (*ohn-mächtig*), that is, they do not make use of power or exercise domination, even as they become more and more active subjects and begin to share in political responsibility.

You are convinced that the messianic goal can be served only by means that are qualitatively of the same kind as the goal. In your view, messianic politics is to be seen in its purest form in the figure of the suffering Servant of God. The conduct of the suffering Servant of God must therefore serve as the model for thinking out and answering the question of political activity.

This summary represents our interpretation of your position. In elaborating its own messianic political ethics, minjung theology leaves behind the prison of "Western" theology and anchors the Christian tradition in the Korean context. Precisely as Western theologians, therefore, we must come to an understanding of what the process of theological contextualization means for the ecumenical dialogue. Permit us, then, as our next step, to summarize what strikes us, as outsiders, about the historical and sociopolitical context of minjung theology.

According to the description of Korean history that is given by representatives of the minjung movement, from earlier centuries down to the present, Korea has repeatedly known periods of agitation in which the minjung have protested against oppression by the political powers that be: in the form sometimes of popular uprisings (the Donghak movement), sometimes of mass demonstrations (the March First Independence movement of 1919), and sometimes of "student rebellions," such as the one that led to the fall of Syngman

Rhee in 1960. These popular movements have all had one thing in common: they have been quickly brought under control by the political authorities and soon suppressed through persecution of their leaders. No popular movement has as yet won a clear and permanent victory over its "antagonist," so that neither the minjung nor any sector of them has thus far reached the point of acquiring political, economic, and military power and becoming in any comprehensive sense an active subject of public responsibility. Even though Suh Nam-dong accepts the thesis of historian Lee Gi-baik that Korean history is to be interpreted as a process of "progressive expansion of the social base of the ruling power," he cannot claim that the minjung have in fact been collaborators at the properly political level.

Owing to the rapid failure of each popular movement, the suffering of the minjung became even greater in the next phase, and this situation continued until a revived hope of a better future led to the next popular movement. The continuing cycle of oppression, prerevolutionary (i.e., primarily nonviolent) protest demonstrations, and still more intense persecution has produced the fundamental Korean experience: the experience of *han* or legitimate outrage at injustice suffered. This almost unparalleled historical experience of the Korean people is probably shared by few other peoples. In the history of the Christian West something similar can be said of the Jewish people, who have been repeatedly persecuted, ghettoized, and threatened with extinction. Typically enough, it is thanks precisely to its messianic (in the original sense of the word) hope that this people has survived all pogroms and, despite its worldwide diaspora, has preserved its identity even to the point of establishing a new state. What we see in Korea, then, is an intrinsic connection between the integrity of the innocent victims of political oppression, the description of the minjung in messianic categories, and a comprehensive critique of power in the political ethics of minjung theology.

If we turn now to reports from other countries and continents, we find it striking that, for example, contextual theologians from Africa or Latin America refer to significantly different experiences of popular movements. For example, many liberation movements in black Africa, after casting off colonial rule and achieving independence, have turned into repressive single-party governments.

First and foremost, however, we think of our own experience in the history of Europe, which is rich in movements that began with a messianic politics but at the historical turning point—the achievement of political success—abruptly turned into blood-thirsty messianisms. At that point, the original minjung movement even became the antagonist of a new minjung. Our recall of these experiences is not meant to play down in any way the yearnings of the oppressed. What impresses us is rather the fact that despite all the yearnings and all the visions of a realized utopian future, messianic politics in Europe has often turned into political messianism.

We think, for example, of the Anabaptist movement at the time of the Reformation: it began as a messianic movement but then—at least in its radical wing, in the North German city of Münster—turned into a bloody political messianism. We think, too, of the longlasting religious wars between Catholic and Protestant territories. What was in part a popular movement at the beginning of the Reformation ended in religio-political struggles for power that brought great suffering on the masses. And we think as well of the secularized forms of political messianism that emerged in the French and Russian revolutions.

As a result of these bitter experiences, concepts reflecting the notion of the "politically feasible" became increasingly important in European social philosophy and theology. Martin Luther, for example, combines hierarchico-patriarchal and populist ideas. On the one hand, in his doctrine of the universal priesthood of all the faithful, he reminds his readers that God thrusts the mighty from their thrones and raises up the lowly, the poor, and the disinherited (Lk. 1:51-53; Mt. 5:3-11); he draws from this the conclusion that those who are lowly by birth should sit with those on high and help in governing (Weimer Edition, 30, 367, 4ff.; 576, 4ff.). On the other hand, he also insists that Christians are obliged to be submissive to the authorities appointed by God. He deliberately maintains the tension between these two positions, whereas later on it has often been abandoned.

In the Calvinist tradition, the biblical idea of covenant and the idea of natural law yielded a theory of a contract between society and its rulers that expected the people, according to their social class, to take a much more active part in things political (consider, for example, the Netherlands).

Since 1945, disillusioned European theologians have seen how difficult it is to produce a democracy in any comprehensive sense of the term. Most blueprints for a theological ethics, therefore, incorporate democratic ideas but typically they do not take the Rousseauian ideal of total democracy as a guide. Instead they see it as the essential task of a theological ethics to critique social reality in light of the classical postulates of democracy. According to H. E. Todt, for example, the role of the church is to serve as a model of "communication that is free of domination" and to "invite others to participate in this." Todt says in this regard: "In a still unredeemed world the political process does not work without a body of law that mediates the claims of individuals to freedom and that can be imposed even by force if need be. It does not work without rulers, because no political community can exist without agencies that are competent to decide in conflicts. At the same time, however, the kingdom of God is there as a reminder that force and violence should be a last resort and that cooperation and consensus should be the foundation of the political process" (*Theologische Realenzyklopädie* 8:446).

Our doubts are obviously not directed at criticisms of the abuse of power. Such criticisms are clearly an imperative for us as well as for you. But in the prevailing ethical ideas of Western theology there is nothing corresponding to the radical criticism of power which you, the minjung theologians, urge. In European theology, rule in some form is presupposed as indispensable, even though it is continually challenged by the vision of the reign of God.

Perhaps our divergent positions may be summed up in this way: Our Western political pragmatism leads to deficiencies from the eschatological standpoint, whereas in the radically eschatological minjung movement we think we see the problems inherent in trying to bring about theological and political utopias.

In this connection we raise the following questions:

1) Does the political vision that flows from hope of God's reign necessarily comprise a radical critique of power and a consequent renunciation of power? Can theological reflection waive the question of legitimate political rule?

2) To what extent can the radically eschatological approach taken by minjung theology not only warrant rebellion against unjust power structures but also be made fruitful for concrete political activity?

3) Has the European tradition, owing to an irresponsible pragmatism, abandoned the eschatological perspective of the Bible for an idealist interpretation of history?

4) Have Western Christians settled too quickly for a "gradualist" approach to the democratization of affluent societies?

Further Theological Themes for Our Dialogue

In offering these critical observations on certain aspects of minjung theology, we are conscious that we stand in a particular theologico-historical tradition, are influenced by it, and are perhaps even captive to it. In fact, we even feel at the moment that our situation here is forcing us to ask whether this tradition can sustain us. We wish once again to insist that we are not measuring minjung theology with the dogmatic yardstick of Western theology; on the other hand, it would be dishonest to hide theological reservations originating in our own history. We hope that our dialogue with you will produce a nuanced clarification, so that we will better understand where we are divided by radically divergent theological positions and where, on the contrary, the differences are simply attributable to perspectival limitations arising from our distinct contexts.

As you are aware, among us the concept of "the people" (*das Volk*) is presently suffering to an exceptional degree from its misuse in our recent German history. This makes it difficult for us to engage in discussion of a "theology of the people." This is not the case in Korea; nonetheless we think our negative experiences important enough to bring them up in ecumenical dialogue.

In the struggle of the churches during the era of National Socialism it was Karl Barth more than any one else who raised his voice in passionate protest against the "popular theology" of the "German Christians," a political party in the church, for he saw this theology as an inadmissible mingling of Christian faith and ideology. In his view this theology was not simply an opportunistic attempt at a *modus vivendi* with the political powers; it was the grotesque expression of a "hyphenated theology" that could appeal to a long and venerable tradition. The first thesis of the Barmen Theological Declaration gave the Confessing Church a classical formulation of its protest: "Jesus Christ, as attested to us in the holy Scriptures, is the One Word of God to which we must listen and which we must trust in and obey in life and in death. We reject this false teaching [of the German Christians], which implies that, apart from and alongside the One Word of God, the Church can and must acknowledge other events and powers, other figures and truths, as God's revelation and the source of its preaching."

We realize today how easily this uncompromisingly christo-centric approach can lead to a ghetto theology that is character-ized by a fatal dualism of church and world, kingdom of God and world history, personal faith and public responsibility. Yet, de-spite this danger of theological narrowness, the theological con-cern formulated at Barmen still seems valid to us today.

It is against this background that we have difficulty with many of your statements as minjung theologians, statements that assert a self-revelation of God before and apart from Jesus Christ and link this self-revelation with historical events. It is true, of course, that a *theological interpretation of history* (including pre-Christian history) can appeal to biblical models. To that extent we can understand the claim that God was at work in Korean his-tory long before the missionaries came ("God was not carried pig-gy-back to Korea by the first missionary": Hyun Young-hak, 54), but we think it a questionable step to turn history into what is in some sense a second source of revelation.

The Fathers at Barmen rightly objected in strong terms to the blasphemy of the "German Christians," who looked upon Hitler as one in whom "Christ, God of Helpers and Redeemers, has inter-vened mightily among us." With the same justification Christian society throughout the world resists those who appeal to God's action in history in order to legitimate their form of rule (for ex-ample, the ideologues of apartheid in South Africa). Even though a clear distinction must be made between repressive and emancip-atory movements, we think nonetheless that we are confronted with what is structurally the same theological approach when, for instance, Suh Nam-dong sees "God's intervention in our histo-ry" in socio-revolutionary movements connected, for example, with Maitreya Buddhism.

Similar questions come to mind in regard to *christology*. We are impressed by your consistent rejection of every form of a *theologia gloriae*. You are in continuity here with the biblical tradition of the Suffering Servant of God, and at the same time you enter terri-tory unexplored by the exegetes when you develop the significance of the *ochlos* [crowd] for the preaching of Jesus. Your study of the Gospel of Mark has shown clearly how closely linked Jesus was with the marginalized crowds in Galilee.

You then carry this insight over into your essays in systematic theology, as you inquire into the theological significance of the marginalized of our day, and specifically of the Korean minjung. By means of the tradition of suffering that is deeply rooted in the Korean people and is expressed in the concept of *han*, you achieve an actualization of the biblical experiences of suffering, such as has not been achieved in European academic theology. You see the suffering Christ in the suffering minjung. He is not only for and with the minjung; he himself is the minjung.

Such insights are important to us, and we accept them gratefully. We have difficulty following you, however, in a series of statements that interpret the Christ event historically and collectively (see Ahn Byung-mu, 138 ff.) and, for example, describe the crucifixion as "the peak in the process of struggle in which the minjung become the protagonists of their own history and destiny" (Suh Nam-dong, 161). We also query the relation established between the biblical Christ and such figures as Chang Il-dam, who is described as "the Jesus of Korea" and a personification of the minjung, and whose "birth, itinerating, preaching of liberation, trial, and execution are the reproduction of the life of Jesus" (179).

From our point of view such an identification of messianic movements or charismatic personages with Jesus of Nazareth is questionable. We think it more appropriate to stick with the biblical language of "following" and avoid talk of "imitation" or reproduction of the work of Christ.

Closely connected with christology are statements in which you assign eschatological attributes to the minjung. We did not overlook your frequent warnings against idealizing the minjung and explaining them in romantic terms (see, e.g., Hyung Young-hak's essay), but you yourselves assign messianic attributes to the minjung as a whole. While you are justified in insisting that the suffering minjung must become the protagonists of their own history, we think it questionable to say that the minjung "must achieve their own salvation" (Suh Nam-dong, 166). Even if minjung is defined as a relational concept and is not identified with a sociological group (e.g., Ahn Byung-mu, 141), many formulations suggest that "the people must achieve their own salvation."

Must not a clear distinction be made here between liberation and redemption? And must there not be a stronger emphasis on the fact that rulers and ruled are equally alienated from God and that both are in need of the forgiveness and redemption which come through the saving work accomplished in Christ? If the radicality of biblical anthropology is to be preserved, then in our opinion the minjung too must be said to be entangled in sin. Talk of "sin" is biblical and not simply "the labels the ruling class uses for the deprived" (Suh Nam-dong, 68).

In closing this section of our letter we would like also to ask about *ecclesiological* concepts in minjung theology. We cannot always determine clearly the distinction being made between "people" and "people of God." This lack of clarity can also be seen in the very title of the German edition of the book we have been frequently citing: *Minjung-Theologie des Volkes Gottes in Sud-Korea* ("People-Theology of the People of God in South Korea"). Even prescinding from a possibly infelicitous German translation we find an inconsistency on this point. It is striking to us how often you speak of *koinonia* and mean by this a community that extends beyond the boundaries of the *Ekklesia*. You appeal in this context to the "Theology of the *Missio Dei*," which in your view "consciously distances itself from the self-assertion of the institutional church" (Ahn Byungmu, "Was ist Minjungtheologie?" *epd Dok* 6a/82, p. 7).

It is undoubtedly correct to say that God does not work solely with and in the church. On the other hand, it also seems clear to us that the church of Jesus Christ has a special role to play. According to Matthew, Jesus defines as his brothers and sisters "those who do the will of my Father in heaven" (Mt 12:50). The mission of the church in the world springs from faith and has for its goal faith in the Lord of the church. We think that from this point of view a clear distinction between "people of God" and "people" must be retained. God cares for the whole of the human race; nonetheless the *Missio Dei* also aims at the gathering of the community. We agree with you in rejecting every form of "ecclesiocentrism" that is satisfied with the *plantatio ecclesiae*, but we are still unclear about the emphasis you place on, and the ecclesiological qualification you give to, various concepts such as *ekklesia, koinonia, ochlos,* to mention a few.

Learning through Ecumenical Dialogue:
Questions Addressed to Us by Minjung Theology

Our questions may strike you as abstract and perhaps as "typically German." They spring neither from a "sociohistorical reflection on texts of the Bible" nor from a current confessional situation of our church. And we can hardly claim to be doing theology in concrete solidarity with the common people, much less with the marginalized of our society. Even though we have plenty of opportunities for focusing on violations of human rights, excessive consumerism, and economic exploitation at both the national and the international levels, our theology often lacks any such relation to praxis. You may therefore find our theological questions academic and irrelevant. Perhaps (and this is the kind of critical question we must put to ourselves) our effort to enter into a dialogue with you is simply an attempt to evade the real challenge of your theology to us by looking only at particular aspects of theology instead of reviewing our whole approach to the discipline.

A comparison of our two approaches gives rise to a question that has repeatedly occupied us in our discussion of minjung theology: How are the theological insights gained in a concrete historical situation to be taken over in a different context?

We have asked ourselves, for example, what meaning *han*, as a collective experience of the Korean people, can have in the German Federal Republic, where there is no comparable tradition of suffering. In our society we usually encounter suffering in an individualized form. We as theologians also lack the kind of identification with the "people" that is possible for you.

From discussion of this and a number of other points we came to the conclusion that it is not possible directly to transfer experiences gained in a different context, much less the theological inferences drawn from those experiences. But while this realization has made us more clearly conscious of the difficulties and limitations of ecumenical dialogue, our study of minjung theology has nonetheless led us to self-criticism and enriching reflection. We would like to illustrate this with the help of the concrete example mentioned in the preceding paragraph.

Just as we have no significant tradition of collective suffering in our history, so too we lack to a large extent a tradition that sets a positive value on the willingness to suffer. We do not interpret suffering as *han*, that is, as suffering that is to be endured in the historical situation and that points forward to resurrection; rather we interpret it individualistically as misfortune that must be overcome. The church has to a great extent adapted itself to this common understanding of suffering, inasmuch as it has built a comprehensive network of social institutions and therapeutic centers that have for their purpose the reduction of suffering.

Under the influence of minjung theology, however, we have come to realize that even among us the "simple folk" do have an awareness of suffering as God's will and a resultant growing ability to accept suffering. This realization has caused us to ask whether the suppression in our theology of what the Bible has to say about suffering and "waiting upon the Lord" may not be a problem peculiar to theologians as a professional class. The prevailing Western theology has in the past had the places of power and knowledge as its "sociological setting" (its *Sitz im Leben*). Could the scriptural witness to a God who renounces power and who suffers have been credibly taught in that setting or have become the basis of a life-style there?

This example shows that for us Western theologians too a promising path may be to take the "religion of the lowly" more seriously than we have in the past. But if we are to enter upon this path, we must share the life and suffering of the lowly. A first step in this direction has been taken in action groups and grassroots communities, the stimulus for which often comes from the experiences of Christians overseas. It is not yet possible to say whether the result will be a "Hjonjang Church" alongside our established Great Churches and a minjung theology alongside our university theology. We do sense, however, that the path you are traveling as minjung theologians is summoning us as well to conversion. Our study of your theology, which grows out of the practice of your faith in solidarity with the Korean minjung, has become a goad for us as theologians. Whether we in our context will achieve a comparable lived faith and a theology reflective of that faith will depend on how deeply we let the goad prick us. The motto, "Think globally, act locally," which Jürgen Moltmann offers in his preface to the German edition of your collection of essays, is a challenge to produce a theology that is at once contextual and ecumenical; this challenge we cannot evade.

We hope that this letter will inaugurate a dialogue with you that will help us to meet the challenge.

We greet you in the communion of our one Lord and Savior.

(Translated by Matthew O'Connell)

A Reply to the Theological Commission of the Protestant Association for World Mission (*Evangelisches Missionswerk*)

by Ahn Byung-mu

We are honored to be permitted to reflect with you more deeply on minjung theology. Your efforts to understand this kind of theology have impressed us a great deal. We are pleased with the positive evaluation you have given minjung theology, even though it is still in its infancy stage and the translations of the term minjung are not yet totally satisfying. We have dealt with your questions together in a small group, and I have been commissioned to share the results with you.

Our reflection process was structured as follows: We translated your questions into Korean, and then sent them to the participants of our minjung theology discussion group. Professor Hyun Young-hak compiled a position statement, with the other members of the group also contributing. In the discussion I assumed the role of moderator, so that I could collect the answers. The discussion was recorded and then transcribed. What I write to you now is based on the statements made by my colleagues.

I will be as faithful as possible to the original meaning, without giving you each participant's exact words. What is not indicated as direct or indirect quotes comes from my summary. With each question you will notice the variety of opinions in our group. Participants in the discussion, besides several junior theologians, were: Dr. Moon Dong-hwan, Professor of Education, Hanschin University; Dr. Suh Kwang-sung, Professor of Systematic Theology, Ewha Womans University; Dr. Hyun Young-hak, Professor of Ethics, Ewha Womans University; Dr. Kim Yong-bock, Presbyterian Theological College; Dr. Koh Chae-shik, Professor of Social Ethics, Hanschin University; and Dr. Kin Chang-nak, Professor of

New Testament Studies, Hanschin University. First of all, we began with the style of theologizing; then we dealt with the individual questions. Lastly, we speculated about the task of theology in the future.

The Overall Structure of the Critique

We have all studied Western theology, mostly in the USA, a few of us in Europe. According to our curriculae vitae, we are Western theology-oriented. Frequently our own thoughts remained underdeveloped; we learned as passive students. We often found ourselves caught in the midst of explanations that, content-wise, we could not digest. A certain reserve capacity still remains, but we cannot find the language to articulate it or to offer appropriate criticism.

For a long time we were totally dominated by the West's logic and mode of inquiry, and we even looked for the answers to our questions in the West. But now our own reality has pushed itself into the foreground, thereby leading us to the realization that we must cast aside what is indigestible. How do we understand the "science" of theology today? This is a very broad topic, and we can only deal with a few of the problems. To our knowledge, science in the Western sense is non-judgmental, objective, neutral, and analytical. Science, according to this understanding, presupposes "pure reason" and is itself a product of the "work of reason." The word "science" (*hak* in Korean and *hangmun* in Chinese) does not necessarily imply a separation of subject and object, nor does *hak* refer specifically to a function of the brain. *Hak* is not only intellectual work, but a comprehensive creative work. Intellectual knowing is only a partial dimension of the entire process. Total human learning is meant here. Value judgments always play a part; objectivity is not the goal.

As Professor Hyun explained, metanoia in Korean does not only mean something ethical or moral, but denotes knowledge as well. Thus, it does not only imply activity, but also refers to understanding and attitude. Knowledge is linked to praxis. The logical, grammatical expression of knowledge is said to be the domain of intellectuals. Simpler people, it is also said, do not lack the knowledge, but frequently the logic to express it. And thus the intellectuals log the findings, determine the results, and thereby stand in danger of dogmatism and a know-it-all mentality. The non-intellectuals do not produce results, do not have a controlled outcome, and would rather follow the way of negation and continue to question further. That only science leads to the truth is in itself a dogmatic assertion. It is exactly the simple people who quest after the truth.

Dr. Kim Young-bock pointed out that Western thinking emphasizes differences, rather than identity. This makes it difficult to conduct a discussion on a positive tone. Frequently, the analytical style of thinking damages the necessary harmony (solidarity). This applies, for example, to political issues such as peace or the world economic order. Common interests are not sought; moreover, you always remain "you," and I always remain "I." In this manner, Western science proves to be an obstacle to moving in solidarity. The subject prepares the object, and thus the difference is demonstrated. For us, value judgments are always implied. "Objective truth," speculative truth, is something unfamiliar to us. The contents of knowledge are bound to the situation. Science tends toward praxis and wants to substantiate action, rather than develop a philosophy of life.

Western theology is very deeply impregnated with dualism. Everyday experiences are separated from religious experiences. The same is also true for the history of the Western church: the church wanted to save its own and therefore took a defensive stance of resistance toward secularization. History and the history of salvation, nation and church, people of God and minjung, had to be absolutely differentiated. This need to divide is almost instinctual. For us this process contradicts belief in creation and God's universality. Dualism is artificial. We seek, above all, unity, not division. Analysis should not split an experience apart; on the contrary, through analysis the interior illumination, the correlated effects of the process of further development, should be comprehended. Not only the special dimension, but also the temporal, should be interpreted. We ourselves were influenced by the West for a long time, but now we reject dualistic differentiation. As Professor Hyun comments, "'God's will,' 'grace,' 'Holy Spirit,' etc., are all words in church talk; but what do they mean in everyday life?" Whenever they are used in daily situations, they are employed to mean that one has engaged all of his or her strength and thereby has experienced the impossible become possible.

"Agape"—is it restricted to Christ? No, included are the everyday experiences (better said, the experiences of everyday life) of the community, the community that renders life possible. It is here that we experience the reality of the teachings of Jesus and touch the realm of inter-religious dialogue. Western Christendom sets Christian religions apart from all other religions. We see therein the vestiges of Christian imperialism. Western theology has called itself scientific and, emphasizing the differences, has devalued other religions. But Buddha teaches *chabi*, Confucius teaches *in*, each differently nuanced. If we review the three concepts, we find that agape, *chabi* and *in* are in harmony with each other. Nygren, for example, differentiated between agape and eros. We do not consider such distinctions realistic or helpful.

Some Western theologians consider Buddhism and Confucianism non-religions, because in these religions faith is missing and God as the object of belief is not present. This is the result of analytical, all too abstractly analytical proceedings. If only one were sensitive and open to searching for similarities, then other results could also be obtained scientifically. Nirvana as final goal means salvation. *Kong* (empty), *mu-hwi* (do nothing), or *mu-ishik* (unconsciousness), concepts of the highest level of this religion, are barred to Western access. The subject-object split does not apply here any longer; it has much more to do with abandonment to the ineffable, the unknowable. Speechlessness is therefore the essence of this belief, a faith, so to speak, of a higher power. In Confucianism there are distinct objects of belief (*schang-ze*). Every people has a belief and objects of belief. For this reason they can understand and accept Christian beliefs. Western theology has only emphasized the absoluteness of Christianity. If, instead, its peculiarity were emphasized, Christianity would then be declared a non-religion (Barth); other religions are systematized in the realm of pre-understanding and thereby devalued.

In the following paragraphs, we consider each of the questions individually, somewhat in the order in which they were submitted to us. Now and then we attempt to address the motive of your questions, as far as we can comprehend it.

Individual Questions

1) Using European experiences as a basis for your question, you skeptically ask about the results of minjung theology. If there were to be a social revolution, then the minjung would no longer be

the suffering class. We would like to challenge your point of view, your perspective. You say that the Anabaptist movement was also a minjung movement, but at the end became a bloody power struggle, a disaster for the people, a negative historical event. Are you not overlooking the fact that a process like this allows the self-confidence of the minjung to grow and power heretofore monopolized to be made relative? We see this kind of process not as a defective development, for these unfortunate periods are transitory moments in a much larger process. Yes, the Tonghak and Samil revolts were squelched, but the suffering strengthened the power of the minjung through an interior process. Are you looking, perhaps, for visible, exterior results too quickly? We are reminded by our own history that Jesus said he had come to bring the sword, not peace. From your point of view, then, even the Jesus-event would have to be negatively assessed.

In your reflections on power and domination you have pointed to the unavoidability of power and might in a yet unredeemed world. That sounds exactly like Luther. In the course of this reflection we will return to the concept of sin, but even now we would like to emphasize the following: Although you are skeptical, we have confidence in the minjung. The presupposition that only might can preserve order, is, in our opinion, a disregard for the human self-governing possibilities of the minjung. Dictators have always justified their oppression with these kinds of anthropological premises. In our interpretation, you are too uncritical of the evil of power, because in your own history Christendom and civil authorities were allied for too long a time. It could be that our criticism of power and force does not fit in with a Western theological ethic; we must ask, however, where the Western ethical concepts come from. Ethics always acquires a broad niche for itself in theology when the eschatological consciousness retreats into the background.

2) You have posed four concrete questions. You ask about the legitimacy of domination. We are suspicious of this way of phrasing the question. How do you understand the concept of "legitimacy"? All empires regard themselves as "legitimate." According to our assessment, however, history does not recognize a single legitimate empire. Not even the rule by the proletariat is legitimate, because it is that in name only. Actually it is a concept that disguises the rule by the party elite. It is also true for Western democracies that political decisions are made by the economic,

scientific and social elite. Without exception these elite determine political events. Yes, democratic governments are better than dictatorships, but true democracies can only be attained through the willingness on the part of the people to suffer (struggle and suffering understood in the sense of an offering).

Korea is a small, weak, often exploited nation. Nevertheless, we are fearful of powerful governments. Confucius, for example, had set forth the legendary Jao-shun era as a model and an ideal, because in that period the hand of government was undetectable. Chang-ja (of Lao-tze's school) went a step further and criticized this ideal government from a more radical standpoint; even this "unnoticeable" form of government was repressive, and the fact that it manipulatively masked its repression is reason for an even sharper critique. Situated, as we are, in the midst of this cultural tradition, we find it necessary to criticize the formulation of your question.

As long as the world exists, there has to be some kind of "order." But "order" is always a disguise for the ambition for power, and to this we are opposed. We raise our voice against every power tactic. We look forward to the autonomy of the minjung, the daughters and sons of God. "Concretely, what will it look like?" you might ask. This question has the same structure, however, as the question about the order of the reign of God.

You ask how our radically eschatological disposition compares in effectiveness to direct political action. Does your question not come out of the context of a historical positivism? Are you not overly interested in visible, demonstrable success? We would like to respond in a twofold manner: 1) God's will leads us in the struggle for justice; there are no accompanying reflections on whether or not success is achieved. 2) Results are not to be found in the visible world. We do not reap everything that we sow. We call to mind the parables of the yeast and the mustard seed. Faith in this context is not naive; on the contrary, traces of the insignificant are present throughout our history.

Yes, in Europe the eschatological, biblical dimension has almost disappeared. We agree with your self-critical admission. We must take care that history is a place of struggle, a process of struggle against the usurpation of power.

Regarding the importance of the "small steps," we agree that in the West too much attention is paid to the consolidation of the existing reality. The ecumenical correlation between well-being on the one side and the disruption of human community on the other is not sufficiently considered.

3) You identify minjung all too easily with "people." A few colleagues were annoyed at this careless identification. Moltmann's volume speaks of the "people of God" in the subtitle. This is totally false. We have never translated minjung as "folk" or "people." We have consciously not defined minjung. A definition would limit the reality and allow the living dimension to be lost. The concept and the reality could turn out to be a contradiction. Your question presumes that you have already understood and defined what minjung is. But precisely in the understanding of minjung bigger differences could lie between you and us.

4) When those of us who promoted minjung theology were driven from the university, we remembered that in the time of the Nazis many German professors were expelled. We thought about the Confessing Church and the Barmen Declaration.

We also thought that we must give witness to Christ as a community, and from these reflections the Galilee Community was born. I reflected on this process in a foreword to sermons from the Galilee Community (published in Japan as *Lord, Come Quickly*):

> In May 1975 eleven professors were expelled from the university. Eight of them were Christian, four were theologians. At that time we thought about Paul Tillich, K.L. Schmidt, Karl Barth, and F. Schultz, who were expelled from the university after 1933. We realized that events such as these not only affected the individuals involved, but had a significance for Korean Christianity as a whole. Whenever we call to mind the history of Germany, we remember the Barmen Declaration and the Confessing Church. As a parallel we founded the Galilee Community. The name is symbolic of the need to witness to our faith by acting as Jesus did, who wept with the minjung and rejoiced with them. Mission must be worked out in engagements of struggle and in the present reality. Our situation has been influenced by the Confessing Church in Germany; at the same time, by taking a critical look, we have seen it in its weakness.
>
> The Barmen theses do not mention whether or not the National Socialist regime was clearly anti-Semitic and chauvinistic. This was the expression of a fugitive stance and was irresponsible—understandable, but false. The Barmen theses

highlighted the concept of *solus Christus*. We see this as positive, because the meaning of *"solus"* is clearly anti-dictatorial. But when this *"solus Christus"* excludes the minjung and turns away from them, then it becomes *"sola ecclesia"* and therefore false! The church may not exist for itself; rather, it must be a Christ-community with the poor and the oppressed. *"Solus Christus"* is also our confession. If it is not to remain an abstract term, then we must act as Jesus did in his identification with the minjung of Galilee. God talk will then be complemented by deeds and action. This action is action with the minjung....

In those years we acted in solidarity with the minjung and were thrown into prison. This was really a blessed experience; we were bodily a part of the minjung. You ask, however, if we do not accept self-manifestations of God outside of the Christ event and see history as the second area of revelation. You inquire, all the while attempting to understand our intentions over the backdrop of Barmen. I would like to ask you in return, "How do you understand revelation?" You have questioned linking God's self-manifestation with historical events. Do you include even the Jesus-event? If not, do you believe that *only* the historical Jesus-event characterizes God's revelation? History, as such, is not for us a second source of revelation. On the other hand, there is no revelation outside of history. The Barmen Declaration attests to Jesus Christ as the only word of God. We see this in another way. We understand Jesus Christ to be the event of God. This event took place in history and continues on in history. We know that Western theology emphasizes the "once and for all" (*ephapax*), so that Christ appears unique, but in so doing, binds the Christ event to a particular time in history and fixes it in the past. We believe that history of itself is not revelation, but Christ as event reveals himself constantly throughout history. The Christ event is therefore central for us, because it is the standard and the criterion for revelation in history. Consequently, from the foregoing, one cannot put Hitler's brutality and policy of separation on the same level with the history of liberation of the minjung. In history we distinguish between the liberation traditions and the powers of oppression. In the liberation movement God's will is revealed in accordance with biblical witness.

You ask if in our opinion God was and also acted beyond and before Christ. Do you mean to say that beyond and before Christ, God would be nothing and thus bound to the Jesus-event? We do not see it this way. Both Hebrew and Christian Scriptures recount the vibrations and currents of salvation. Nothing limits God's salvific design. Often in Western theology the representation of the unknown God in Paul's discourse at the Areopagus is considered a scandal. In this manner Christianity makes itself absolute through the wrong means. At the same time, God as Lord of the world and universe gets lost. This tendency has ongoing influence, if God does not exist "before" and "outside of." If the Christ event is bound to the happenings of 2000 years ago, then the cross and death of Jesus signal the end.

For us, however, the present, acting Christ is important. How does Christ exist in history with us today? That is our question. We vigorously object to a word of God theology in which the sermon proclamation is the only place of revelation and its only realization. We believe that suffering is a main biblical theme. It begins with the exodus: the suffering minjung are historically freed. The same is true for the Christian Scriptures: Jesus chooses in Galilee the battlefield of reality as his place of mission, which leads to his murder in Jerusalem. The kerygma is right: the cross is the center of this event. We think that faith in the resurrection is a confession of the saving exodus God. The gospels, especially the Gospel of Mark, attest not to past suffering, but to the suffering Christ in present day men and women. In this sense the (a-theistic) description of the passion of Jesus is of great significance to us, as is Matthew 25. We often refer to Heb. 13:12-14 and believe we can also interpret the pauline theology of the cross in this sense. Paul confesses, in the midst of suffering, the present Christ; the suffering of the apostle makes him one with and identical to his Lord.

You have asked if Suh Nam-dong actually saw Christ in the Kim Chi Ha figure of Chang Il-dam, or how Christ and this figure are related. We ask in return if you see Christ only as a person and have him frozen in the past. Chang Il-dam is not identical to Christ as a person, but the Jesus-event continues to act gradually in this event. You have emphasized that it would be wrong to attempt an *imitatio Christi*; "following Christ" is the theological mandate. But ironically, if we emphasize "following," we must give prominence to people with their own accomplishments. According to our understanding Jesus and the Jesus event continue and take the initiative, so to speak, in the happenings of our time. The *imitatio* encompasses our activity and within it Jesus himself remains "initiator."

5) Finally the question about sin. You ask if, in our opinion, the minjung can redeem themselves; if the minjung are, subsequently, sinless. It appears to us that the subject-object pattern becomes evident once again with this type of questioning. Savior and those to be saved; God as the subject of salvation and human beings as the object of salvation: This scheme lurks in the background and has shaped us for a long time. But the story of salvation is all-encompassing and does not carry with it this division of action and passivity.

To be saved is not a passive process. Human effort and the gift of grace are not to be viewed as separate. Grace is central and religiously important; but human endeavor cannot be separated from it. Both are one, the same in different languages. Yes, the minjung have the potential of liberation. We do not consider the minjung either morally or ethically "sinless," and we are not glossing over anything. We acknowledge the ordinary depravity of the minjung; ethically and morally the simple people can often be even worse than others. Yet, we have had the amazing experience again and again that among the minjung something akin to self-transcendence can occur. By this we mean especially the minjung's readiness to expend their efforts, their non-laziness and their willingness for sacrifice. To us this is a phenomenon. We cannot analyze such occurrences according to the subject-object schema.

They do not reckon with the word "sin" primarily in the parlance of the ruling class, but according to its use in the Bible. We believe that theologians are correct in demanding a current translation of biblical language. Biblical concepts and the biblical message can and should be interpreted under social scientific aspects. As far as we have understood, the prophets assailed the wealthy and those in power because of their sins and their injustice. The exploitation and the oppression of the minjung is a sin. It is *exousia*, or a misuse of power, that contradicts the divine plan. This lording of power over other men and women is a sin. Naturally we also see other "sins" in their ethical, juridical and ritualistic aspects. But the condemnation of these types of "sins" comes from the dominant value system. This value system and concept of sin are meant to maintain the status quo. Precisely during David's kingship the following development became evident: The original intention of the word of God was given a new interpretation and was misused as a juridical basis for the glorification of those in power. One can also read the history of the church in the same manner; the church often became a value unto itself. In this context the dogma of original sin was formulated and refined, and served the purposes of those interested in theological order and ecclesiastical security. In the process, the name of God was used falsely.

We must keep before our eyes the victim when we speak of "sin." The crucial question of who becomes the victim of corresponding concepts of sin is more important than the concept of sin itself. Jesus and Paul support us here. Jesus never examined or denounced the sins of the minjung, but he did make public the sins of the Pharisees in a big way. He sharply criticized the powerful for wanting to define sinfulness. Jesus broke through the legal system and it led to his death.

We should also reflect on the concept of sin in Paul. Without the law there was no motive for sin (Rom. 7:7). This very understanding of sin in Paul, we realize, was an attack on the power holders' theology of sin. Sin is something that must be brought to an end, according to Paul, because the law itself has come to an end. Of course, we see that Paul is emphasizing the connection between sin and law. All people live under sin, because one person sinned. But the entire argument of Paul is directed toward salvation and redemption; he is absolutely not fixated on sin. Everybody, both the domineering class and the minjung, is in need of this healing.

6) You emphasize that Christ gave the church special responsibilities and functions, but on the other hand you concede that God does not work only through the church. We do not deny this. But we return the question: Which church do you mean? Matthew backs you up: "Anyone who does the will of my Father in heaven, he is my brother and sister and mother" (Mt. 12:50). But bear in mind that the church must genuinely fulfill the will of God. In the biblical quotations that you have cited Jesus actually addresses his disciples. It is different in the synoptic parallel verses in Mark. There Jesus uses these words to speak to the crowds. Is this not proof that the difference between "people of God" and minjung is untenable? And we ask, do you not seek to preserve the place of prominence of the church? Who is it who does the will of God? Is it necessarily the baptized, those who attend religious services, those who confess Christ? Is not security—ritualistic, religious security—the issue for them? Does Jesus not mean even first of all those who give of

themselves in the struggle for justice, without naming Christ or belonging to the church? We do not believe that exterior standard can be the judge of anything in these matters. "The people of God" cannot be analyzed from the outside. For this reason the distinction between the visible and the invisible church is well made.

We want to close by expressing our feeling of respect for your willingness to dialogue and your efforts to understand our theological thought. You said that you yourself had no experience with the kind of suffering we spoke about; thus, it is difficult for you to understand *han* (as an expression of collective suffering). It is difficult for us to understand how you can say that you have no collective experience of suffering after the Second World War. Did the entire European world not suffer dreadfully? Did the Jews not suffer collectively and did that not happen in the collective German name? How can that all be put aside in your theology?

The Bible is the source of all theology. In the Bible, collective suffering is the main theme. How can one understand the Bible without experiencing this main theme? Yes, for a long time we have understood the Jesus-event narrowly and individualistically. But insofar as we see ourselves standing on the battlefield of the people, we understand the Bible, the story of Exodus and the fulfillment of the promises of the Jesus-event in a new way. All of this is one collectively related happening. You say that in your situation well-being and non-suffering are predominant. Is it at all possible to witness to a suffering God in this context? Do we recognize here a sigh of resignation with respect to the possibility of theologizing? If you keep on theologizing, it can no longer be to maintain a certain well-being and the status quo. You have expressed that it would be hardly possible from a European context to understand theology in other contexts. That would be a tragedy, because then we could no longer understand Jesus and Paul, and ecumenism would be impossible.

But we believe you are not giving in to resignation. We believe in the possibilities of dialogue and understanding. We are capable of overcoming cultural, political and economic barriers. Pentecost is the sign for this, and marvelous events such as this one happen now and continually, working on in us and our efforts. We continue this event.

I wish to send my sincerest regards.

(Translated by Marianne Smith Varni)

About the Contributors

Robert McAfee Brown is Professor Emeritus of Theology and Ethics at Pacific School of Religion in Berkeley, California. A recognized interpreter of liberation theologies of the Third World, Dr. Brown is the author of *Theology in a New Key: Responding to Liberation Themes* (1978), *Unexpected News: Reading the Bible with Third World Eyes* (1984), and *Spirituality and Liberation: Overcoming the Great Fall* (1988), all published by Westminster. Through his involvement with the World Council of Churches, he has traveled extensively throughout Latin America, and has also visited Africa and Southeast Asia.

John B. Cobb, Jr., a leading exponent of process theology, is Ingraham Professor of Theology at the School of Theology at Claremont, California. He is the author of numerous books, including *Process Theology as Political Theology* (Westminster, 1982) and *Beyond Dialogue: Toward a Mutual Transformation of Christianity and Buddhism* (Fortress, 1982). Born in Japan, he is widely familiar with Asian religions, and has for many years been in constructive dialogue with Third World liberation theologies.

Harvey Cox is Victor S. Thomas Professor of Divinity at Harvard Divinity School, and teaches religious studies at Harvard University. He is the author of numerous books, including *The Secular City* (Macmillan, 1965), *Religion in the Secular City* (Simon and Schuster, 1984), and has in recent years explored the myriad implications of Third World theologies as his work, *Many Mansions: A Christian's Encounter with Other Faiths* (Beacon, 1988) illustrates.

Kwesi A. Dickson is Professor of Old Testament Studies and Modern Theological Trends at the University of Ghana. He was the first Chairman of the West African Association of Theological Institutions, and a founding member of the Ecumenical Association of Third World Theologians. His many publications include *Theology in Africa* (Orbis Books, 1984) and *Biblical Revelation and African Beliefs* (Lutterworth, 1969).

Kosuke Koyama is John D. Rockefeller, Jr., Professor of Ecumenics and World Christianity at Union Theological Seminary in New York City. A minister of The United Church of Christ, Dr. Koyama holds graduate degrees in theology from Princeton University, Drew University, and Tokyo Union Theological Seminary, and served as a missioner in Thailand for eight years. He has participated in the Asian Missionary Consultation of the Christian Conference of Asia, and has held many leadership positions with the World Council of Churches. His many books, including *No Handle on the Cross* (1975), *Waterbuffalo Theology* (1974), and *Mount Fuji and Mount Sinai* (1984), all published by SCM and Orbis Books, have received wide acclaim for their attempt to discern the meaning of the Christian experience within an Asian setting.

Jung Young Lee is uniquely qualified to edit a volume on Korean minjung theology. A native of Korea, Dr. Lee is chairperson of the religious studies department at the University of North Dakota. He was the Fulbright-Hays Senior Scholar at Seoul National University and Ewha Womans University in Korea in 1977, and, since 1979, has served as President of the Korean Society for Religious Studies in North America. He is the author of several books, including *The Theology of Change* (Orbis Books, 1979) and *Sermons to the Twelve* (Abingdon, 1988).

José Míguez Bonino is one of the foremost liberation theologians of Latin America. He is Emeritus Professor of Systematic Theology, Protestant Institute for Higher Theological Education, Buenos Aires, Argentina, and has served as Co-President of the World Council of Churches. His many publications include *Doing Theology in a Revolutionary Situation* (Fortress, 1975), *Toward a Christian Political Ethics* (Fortress, 1983), and, as editor, *Faces of Jesus: Latin American Christologies* (Orbis Books, 1984).

George Ogle is Program Director for the Department of Social and Economic Justice at the General Board of Church and Society, the United Methodist Church, in Washington, D.C. He served for fifteen years as a missionary in South Korea in educational and evangelical ministry to industrial workers. In 1974, he was arrested by the Korean CIA and expelled from the country for his support of eight men who were arrested and tortured by South Korea's military dictatorship. Upon returning to the USA, Dr. Ogle assumed a teaching position at Candler School of Theology in Atlanta before moving to his present position in Washington, D.C.

J. Deotis Roberts is Distinguished Professor of Philosophical Theology at Eastern Baptist Theological Seminary in Philadelphia. He is author of *Black Theology in Dialogue* (1987) and *Roots of a Black Future: Family and Church* (1980), both published by Westminster. He has traveled extensively in Asia, including South Korea, and has a deep interest in Third World theologies and their relation to black theology in the USA.

Letty M. Russell is Professor of Theology at Yale Divinity School. She was ordained to the ministry in 1958 by The United Presbyterian Church, USA, and served as pastor and educator in the East Harlem Protestant Parish for seventeen years. She has edited *Feminist Interpretation of the Bible* (Westminster, 1985), and published *Household of Freedom: Authority in Feminist Theology* (Westminster, 1987). She is active in the Commission on Faith and Order of the National Council of Churches and the World Council of Churches.

C.S. Song is Professor of Theology and Asian Cultures at Pacific School of Religion in Berkeley, California, and is Regional Professor of Theology at the Southeast Asia Graduate School of Theology. A vibrant and creative thinker, he is the author of many works, including *Tell Us Our Names: Story Theology from an Asian Perspective* (1984), and *Theology from the Womb of Asia* (1986), both published by Orbis Books. In 1983, at the request of the National Council of Churches in Korea, Song participated in a conference addressing the future of minjung theology, held at the Mission Education Institute in Seoul, South Korea.

Select Bibliography

Billings, Peggy, ed. *Fire beneath the Frost*. New York: Friendship Press, 1984.

Christian Conference of Asia, *CTC Bulletin* (Bulletin of the Commision on the Theological Concerns). Singapore, Vol. 5, No. 3–Vol. 6, No. 1, December 1984-April 1985.

Cho Wha-soon. *Let the Weak Be Strong: A Woman's Struggle for Justice*. Oak Park, Ill.: Meyer-Stone Books, 1988.

Commission on Theological Concerns of the Christian Conference of Asia. *Minjung Theology: People as the Subjects of History*. Maryknoll, N.Y., London, Singapore: Orbis Books, Zed Press, Christian Conference of Asia, 1983.

Dong Unmo, ed. *Korean-American Relations at Crossroads*. Princeton Junction, N.J.: Association of Korean Christian Scholars in North America, 1982.

Hyun Young-hak. "The Cripple's Dance and Minjung Theology" in *Ching Feng*, Vol. 28, No. 1, 1985.

Kim Chi Ha. *The Gold-Crowned Jesus and Other Writings*. Ed. by Chong Sun-kim and Shelly Killen. Maryknoll, N.Y.: Orbis Books, 1978.

Lee Sang-hyun, ed. *Essays on Korean Heritage and Christianity*. Princeton Junction, N.J.: Association of Korean Christian Scholars in North America, 1984.

Moltmann, Jürgen, ed. *Minjung-Theologie des Volkes Gottes in Südkorea*. Neukirchen-Vluyn, West Germany: Neukirchener Verlag, 1984.

Moon Hee-suk Cyris. *A Korean Minjung Theology: An Old Testament Perspective*. Maryknoll, N.Y., Hong Kong: Orbis Books, Plough Publications, 1985.

Park Sung-ho Andrew. "Minjung Theology: A Korean Contextual Theology," in *Pacific Theological Review*, Winter 1985.

Phillips, Earl H. and Yu Eui-Young, eds. *Religion in Korea*. Los Angeles: Center for Korean-American and Korean Studies, 1982.

Tabuch Fumio, "Der Katholische Dichter Kim Chi Ha als Narrativer Theologe im Asia Tischen Kontext" in *Zeitschrift fur Missionswissenschaft und Religionswissenschaft*. Vol. 69, No.1–24, January 1985.